INSIGHT PUBLICA®

INSIGHT PUBLICA

Nadakkave, Kozhikode, Kerala, India
+91 4954020666 | +91 9400737475
www.insightpublica.com
e-mail: insightpublica@gmail.com

Major Barbara

Bernard Shaw

This Insight Edition: March 2020

ISBN 978-93-89155-44-0

Published by
Insightinpublica Publishers Pvt. Ltd.
Printed at Repro India Limited, India

Major Barbara

Bernard Shaw

INSIGHT PUBLICA

ACT I

It is after dinner on a January night, in the library in Lady Britomart Undershaft's house in Wilton Crescent. A large and comfortable settee is in the middle of the room, upholstered in dark leather. A person sitting on it [it is vacant at present] would have, on his right, Lady Britomart's writing table, with the lady herself busy at it; a smaller writing table behind him on his left; the door behind him on Lady Britomart's side; and a window with a window seat directly on his left. Near the window is an armchair.

Lady Britomart is a woman of fifty or thereabouts, well dressed and yet careless of her dress, well bred and quite reckless of her breeding, well mannered and yet appallingly outspoken and indifferent to the opinion of her interlocutory, amiable and yet peremptory, arbitrary, and high-tempered to the last bearable degree, and withal a very typical managing matron of the upper class, treated as a naughty child until she grew into a scolding mother, and finally settling down with plenty of practical ability and worldly experience, limited in the oddest way with domestic and class limitations, conceiving the universe exactly as if it were a large house in Wilton Crescent, though handling her corner of it very effectively on that assumption, and being quite enlightened and liberal as to the books in the library, the pictures on the walls, the music in the portfolios, and the articles in the papers.

Her son, Stephen, comes in. He is a gravely correct young man under 25, taking himself very seriously, but still in some awe of his mother, from childish habit and bachelor shyness rather than from any weakness of character.

STEPHEN. What's the matter?

LADY BRITOMART. Presently, Stephen.

Stephen submissively walks to the settee and sits down. He takes up The Speaker.

LADY BRITOMART. Don't begin to read, Stephen. I shall require all your attention.

STEPHEN. It was only while I was waiting—

LADY BRITOMART. Don't make excuses, Stephen. [He puts down The Speaker]. Now! [She finishes her writing; rises; and comes to the settee]. I have not kept you waiting very long, I think.

STEPHEN. Not at all, mother.

LADY BRITOMART. Bring me my cushion. [He takes the cushion from the chair at the desk and arranges it for her as she sits down on the settee]. Sit down. [He sits down and fingers his tie nervously]. Don't fiddle with your tie, Stephen: there is nothing the matter with it.

STEPHEN. I beg your pardon. [He fiddles with his watch chain instead].

LADY BRITOMART. Now are you attending to me, Stephen?

STEPHEN. Of course, mother.

LADY BRITOMART. No: it's not of course. I want something much more than your everyday matter-of-course attention. I am going to speak to you very seriously, Stephen. I wish you would let that chain alone.

STEPHEN [hastily relinquishing the chain] Have I done anything to annoy you, mother? If so, it was quite unintentional.

LADY BRITOMART [astonished] Nonsense! [With some remorse] My poor boy, did you think I was angry with you?

STEPHEN. What is it, then, mother? You are making me very uneasy.

LADY BRITOMART [squaring herself at him rather aggressively] Stephen: may I ask how soon you intend to realize that you are a grown-up man, and that I am only a woman?

STEPHEN [amazed] Only a—

LADY BRITOMART. Don't repeat my words, please: It is a most aggravating habit. You must learn to face life seriously, Stephen. I really cannot bear the whole burden of our family affairs any longer. You must advise me: you must assume the responsibility.

STEPHEN. I!

LADY BRITOMART. Yes, you, of course. You were 24 last June. You've been at Harrow and Cambridge. You've been to India and Japan. You must know a lot of things now; unless you have wasted your time most scandalously. Well, advise me.

STEPHEN [much perplexed] You know I have never interfered in the household—

LADY BRITOMART. No: I should think not. I don't want you to order the dinner.

STEPHEN. I mean in our family affairs.

LADY BRITOMART. Well, you must interfere now; for they are getting quite beyond me.

STEPHEN [troubled] I have thought sometimes that perhaps I ought; but really, mother, I know so little about them; and what I do know is so painful—it is so impossible to mention some things to you—[he stops, ashamed].

LADY BRITOMART. I suppose you mean your father.

STEPHEN [almost inaudibly] Yes.

LADY BRITOMART. My dear: we can't go on all our lives not mentioning him. Of course you were quite right not to open the subject until I asked you to; but you are old enough now to be taken into my confidence, and to help me to deal with him about the girls.

STEPHEN. But the girls are all right. They are engaged.

LADY BRITOMART [complacently] Yes: I have made a very good match for

Sarah. Charles Lomax will be a millionaire at 35. But that is ten years ahead; and in the meantime his trustees cannot under the terms of his father's will allow him more than 800 pounds a year.

STEPHEN. But the will says also that if he increases his income by his own exertions, they may double the increase.

LADY BRITOMART. Charles Lomax's exertions are much more likely to decrease his income than to increase it. Sarah will have to find at least another 800 pounds a year for the next ten years; and even then they will be as poor as church mice. And what about Barbara? I thought Barbara was going to make the most brilliant career of all of you. And what does she do? Joins the Salvation Army; discharges her maid; lives on a pound a week; and walks in one evening with a professor of Greek whom she has picked up in the street, and who pretends to be a Salvationist, and actually plays the big drum for her in public because he has fallen head over ears in love with her.

STEPHEN. I was certainly rather taken aback when I heard they were engaged. Cusins is a very nice fellow, certainly: nobody would ever guess that he was born in Australia; but—

LADY BRITOMART. Oh, Adolphus Cusins will make a very good husband. After all, nobody can say a word against Greek: it stamps a man at once as an educated gentleman. And my family, thank Heaven, is not a pig-headed Tory one. We are Whigs, and believe in liberty. Let snobbish people say what they please: Barbara shall marry, not the man they like, but the man I like.

STEPHEN. Of course I was thinking only of his income. However, he is not likely to be extravagant.

LADY BRITOMART. Don't be too sure of that, Stephen. I know your quiet, simple, refined, poetic people like Adolphus—quite content with the best of everything! They cost more than your extravagant people, who are always as mean as they are second rate. No: Barbara will need at least 2000 pounds a year. You see it means two additional households. Besides, my dear, you must marry soon. I don't approve of the present fashion of philandering bachelors and late marriages; and I am trying to arrange something for you.

STEPHEN. It's very good of you, mother; but perhaps I had better arrange that for myself.

LADY BRITOMART. Nonsense! you are much too young to begin matchmaking: you would be taken in by some pretty little nobody. Of course I don't mean that you are not to be consulted: you know that as well as I do. [Stephen closes his lips and is silent]. Now don't sulk, Stephen.

STEPHEN. I am not sulking, mother. What has all this got to do with—with—with my father?

LADY BRITOMART. My dear Stephen: where is the money to come from? It is easy enough for you and the other children to live on my income as long as we are in the same house; but I can't keep four families in four separate houses. You know how poor my father is: he has barely seven thousand a year now; and really, if he were not the Earl of Stevenage, he would have to give up society. He can do nothing for us: he says, naturally enough, that it is absurd that he should be asked to provide for the children of a man who is rolling in money. You see, Stephen, your father must be fabulously wealthy, because there is always a war going on somewhere.

STEPHEN. You need not remind me of that, mother. I have hardly ever opened a newspaper in my life without seeing our name in it. The Undershaft torpedo! The Undershaft quick firers! The Undershaft ten inch! the Undershaft disappearing rampart gun! the Undershaft submarine! and now the Undershaft aerial battleship! At Harrow they called me the Woolwich Infant. At Cambridge it was the same. A little brute at King's who was always trying to get up revivals, spoilt my Bible—your first birthday present to me—by writing under my name, "Son and heir to Undershaft and Lazarus, Death and Destruction Dealers: address, Christendom and Judea." But that was not so bad as the way I was kowtowed to everywhere because my father was making millions by selling cannons.

LADY BRITOMART. It is not only the cannons, but the war loans that Lazarus arranges under cover of giving credit for the cannons. You know, Stephen, it's perfectly scandalous. Those two men, Andrew Undershaft and Lazarus, positively have Europe under their thumbs. That is why your father is able to behave as he does. He is above the law. Do you think Bismarck or Gladstone or Disraeli could have openly defied every social and moral obligation all their lives as your father has? They simply wouldn't have dared. I asked Gladstone to take it up. I asked The Times to take it up. I asked the Lord Chamberlain to take it up. But it was just like asking them to declare war on the Sultan. They WOULDN'T. They said they couldn't touch him. I believe they were afraid.

STEPHEN. What could they do? He does not actually break the law.

LADY BRITOMART. Not break the law! He is always breaking the law. He broke the law when he was born: his parents were not married.

STEPHEN. Mother! Is that true?

LADY BRITOMART. Of course it's true: that was why we separated.

STEPHEN. He married without letting you know this!

LADY BRITOMART [rather taken aback by this inference] Oh no. To do Andrew justice, that was not the sort of thing he did. Besides, you know the Undershaft motto: Unashamed. Everybody knew.

STEPHEN. But you said that was why you separated.

LADY BRITOMART. Yes, because he was not content with being a foundling himself: he wanted to disinherit you for another foundling. That was what I couldn't stand.

STEPHEN [ashamed] Do you mean for—for—for—

LADY BRITOMART. Don't stammer, Stephen. Speak distinctly.

STEPHEN. But this is so frightful to me, mother. To have to speak to you about such things!

LADY BRITOMART. It's not pleasant for me, either, especially if you are still so childish that you must make it worse by a display of embarrassment. It is only in the middle classes, Stephen, that people get into a state of dumb helpless horror when they find that there are wicked people in the world. In our class, we have to decide what is to be done with wicked people; and nothing should disturb our self possession. Now ask your question properly.

STEPHEN. Mother: you have no consideration for me. For Heaven's sake either treat me as a child, as you always do, and tell me nothing at all; or tell me everything and let me take it as best I can.

LADY BRITOMART. Treat you as a child! What do you mean? It is most unkind and ungrateful of you to say such a thing. You know I have never treated any of you as children. I have always made you my companions and friends, and allowed you perfect freedom to do and say whatever you liked, so long as you liked what I could approve of.

STEPHEN [desperately] I daresay we have been the very imperfect children of a very perfect mother; but I do beg you to let me alone for once, and tell me about this horrible business of my father wanting to set me aside for another son.

LADY BRITOMART [amazed] Another son! I never said anything of the kind. I never dreamt of such a thing. This is what comes of interrupting me.

STEPHEN. But you said—

LADY BRITOMART [cutting him short] Now be a good boy, Stephen, and listen to me patiently. The Undershafts are descended from a foundling in the parish of St. Andrew Undershaft in the city. That was long ago, in the reign of James the First. Well, this foundling was adopted by an armorer and gun-maker. In the course of time the foundling succeeded to the business; and from some notion of gratitude, or some vow or something, he adopted another foundling, and left the business to him. And that foundling did the same. Ever since that, the cannon business has always been left to an adopted foundling named Andrew Undershaft.

STEPHEN. But did they never marry? Were there no legitimate sons?

LADY BRITOMART. Oh yes: they married just as your father did; and they were rich enough to buy land for their own children and leave them well provided for. But they always adopted and trained some foundling to succeed them in the business; and of course they always quarrelled with their wives furiously over it. Your father was adopted in that way; and he pretends to consider himself bound to keep up the tradition and adopt somebody to leave the business to. Of course I was not going to stand that. There may have been some reason for it when the Undershafts could only marry women in their own class, whose sons were not fit to govern great estates. But there could be no excuse for passing over my son.

STEPHEN [dubiously] I am afraid I should make a poor hand of managing a cannon foundry.

LADY BRITOMART. Nonsense! you could easily get a manager and pay him a salary.

STEPHEN. My father evidently had no great opinion of my capacity.

LADY BRITOMART. Stuff, child! you were only a baby: it had nothing to do with your capacity. Andrew did it on principle, just as he did every perverse and wicked thing on principle. When my father remonstrated, Andrew actually told him to his face that history tells us of only two successful institutions: one the Undershaft firm, and the other the Roman Empire under the Antonines. That was because the Antonine emperors all adopted their successors. Such rubbish! The Stevenages are as good as the Antonines, I hope; and you are a Stevenage. But that was Andrew all over. There you have the man! Always clever and unanswerable when he was defending nonsense and wickedness: always awkward and sullen when he had to behave sensibly and decently!

STEPHEN. Then it was on my account that your home life was broken up, mother. I am sorry.

LADY BRITOMART. Well, dear, there were other differences. I really cannot bear an immoral man. I am not a Pharisee, I hope; and I should not have minded his merely doing wrong things: we are none of us perfect. But your father didn't exactly do wrong things: he said them and thought them: that was what was so dreadful. He really had a sort of religion of wrongness just as one doesn't mind men practising immorality so long as they own that they are in the wrong by preaching morality; so I couldn't forgive Andrew for preaching immorality while he practised morality. You would all have grown up without principles, without any knowledge of right and wrong, if he had been in the house. You know, my dear, your father was a very attractive man in some ways. Children did not dislike him;

and he took advantage of it to put the wickedest ideas into their heads, and make them quite unmanageable. I did not dislike him myself: very far from it; but nothing can bridge over moral disagreement.

STEPHEN. All this simply bewilders me, mother. People may differ about matters of opinion, or even about religion; but how can they differ about right and wrong? Right is right; and wrong is wrong; and if a man cannot distinguish them properly, he is either a fool or a rascal: that's all.

LADY BRITOMART [touched] That's my own boy [she pats his cheek]! Your father never could answer that: he used to laugh and get out of it under cover of some affectionate nonsense. And now that you understand the situation, what do you advise me to do?

STEPHEN. Well, what can you do?

LADY BRITOMART. I must get the money somehow.

STEPHEN. We cannot take money from him. I had rather go and live in some cheap place like Bedford Square or even Hampstead than take a farthing of his money.

LADY BRITOMART. But after all, Stephen, our present income comes from Andrew.

STEPHEN [shocked] I never knew that.

LADY BRITOMART. Well, you surely didn't suppose your grandfather had anything to give me. The Stevenages could not do everything for you. We gave you social position. Andrew had to contribute something. He had a very good bargain, I think.

STEPHEN [bitterly] We are utterly dependent on him and his cannons, then!

LADY BRITOMART. Certainly not: the money is settled. But he provided it. So you see it is not a question of taking money from him or not: it is simply a question of how much. I don't want any more for myself.

STEPHEN. Nor do I.

LADY BRITOMART. But Sarah does; and Barbara does. That is, Charles Lomax and Adolphus Cusins will cost them more. So I must put my pride in my pocket and ask for it, I suppose. That is your advice, Stephen, is it not?

STEPHEN. No.

LADY BRITOMART [sharply] Stephen!

STEPHEN. Of course if you are determined—

LADY BRITOMART. I am not determined: I ask your advice; and I am waiting for it. I will not have all the responsibility thrown on my shoulders.

STEPHEN [obstinately] I would die sooner than ask him for another penny.

LADY BRITOMART [resignedly] You mean that I must ask him. Very well, Stephen: It shall be as you wish. You will be glad to know that your grandfather concurs. But he thinks I ought to ask Andrew to come here and see the girls. After all, he must have some natural affection for them.

STEPHEN. Ask him here!!!

LADY BRITOMART. Do not repeat my words, Stephen. Where else can I ask him?

STEPHEN. I never expected you to ask him at all.

LADY BRITOMART. Now don't tease, Stephen. Come! you see that it is necessary that he should pay us a visit, don't you?

STEPHEN [reluctantly] I suppose so, if the girls cannot do without his money.

LADY BRITOMART. Thank you, Stephen: I knew you would give me the right advice when it was properly explained to you. I have asked your father to come this evening. [Stephen bounds from his seat] Don't jump, Stephen: it fidgets me.

STEPHEN [in utter consternation] Do you mean to say that my father is coming here to-night—that he may be here at any moment?

LADY BRITOMART [looking at her watch] I said nine. [He gasps. She rises]. Ring the bell, please. [Stephen goes to the smaller writing table; presses a button on it; and sits at it with his elbows on the table and his head in his hands, outwitted and overwhelmed]. It is ten minutes to nine yet; and I have to prepare the girls. I asked Charles Lomax and Adolphus to dinner on purpose that they might be here. Andrew had better see them in case he should cherish any delusions as to their being capable of supporting their wives. [The butler enters: Lady Britomart goes behind the settee to speak to him]. Morrison: go up to the drawingroom and tell everybody to come down here at once. [Morrison withdraws. Lady Britomart turns to Stephen]. Now remember, Stephen, I shall need all your countenance and authority. [He rises and tries to recover some vestige of these attributes]. Give me a chair, dear. [He pushes a chair forward from the wall to where she stands, near the smaller writing table. She sits down; and he goes to the armchair, into which he throws himself]. I don't know how Barbara will take it. Ever since they made her a major in the Salvation Army she has developed a propensity to have her own way and order people about which quite cows me sometimes. It's not ladylike: I'm sure I don't know where she picked it up. Anyhow, Barbara shan't bully me; but still it's just as well that your father should be here before she has time to refuse to meet him or make a fuss. Don't look nervous, Stephen, it will only encourage Barbara to make difficulties. I am nervous enough, goodness knows; but I don't show it.

Sarah and Barbara come in with their respective young men, Charles Lomax and Adolphus Cusins. Sarah is slender, bored, and mundane. Barbara is robuster, jollier, much more energetic. Sarah is fashionably dressed: Barbara is in Salvation Army uniform. Lomax, a young man about town, is like many other young men about town. He is affected with a frivolous sense of humor which plunges him at the most inopportune moments into paroxysms of imperfectly suppressed laughter. Cusins is a spectacled student, slight, thin haired, and sweet voiced, with a more complex form of Lomax's complaint. His sense of humor is intellectual and subtle, and is complicated by an appalling temper. The lifelong struggle of a benevolent temperament and a high conscience against impulses of inhuman ridicule and fierce impatience has set up a chronic strain which has visibly wrecked his constitution. He is a most implacable, determined, tenacious, intolerant person who by mere force of character presents himself as—and indeed actually is—considerate, gentle, explanatory, even mild and apologetic, capable possibly of murder, but not of cruelty or coarseness. By the operation of some instinct which is not merciful enough to blind him with the illusions of love, he is obstinately bent on marrying Barbara. Lomax likes Sarah and thinks it will be rather a lark to marry her. Consequently he has not attempted to resist Lady Britomart's arrangements to that end.

All four look as if they had been having a good deal of fun in the drawing-room. The girls enter first, leaving the swains outside. Sarah comes to the settee. Barbara comes in after her and stops at the door.

BARBARA. Are Cholly and Dolly to come in?

LADY BRITOMART [forcibly] Barbara: I will not have Charles called Cholly: the vulgarity of it positively makes me ill.

BARBARA. It's all right, mother. Cholly is quite correct nowadays. Are they to come in?

LADY BRITOMART. Yes, if they will behave themselves.

BARBARA [through the door] Come in, Dolly, and behave yourself.

Barbara comes to her mother's writing table. Cusins enters smiling, and wanders towards Lady Britomart.

SARAH [calling] Come in, Cholly. [Lomax enters, controlling his features very imperfectly, and places himself vaguely between Sarah and Barbara].

LADY BRITOMART [peremptorily] Sit down, all of you. [They sit. Cusins crosses to the window and seats himself there. Lomax takes a chair. Barbara sits at the writing table and Sarah on the settee]. I don't in the least know what you are laughing at, Adolphus. I am surprised at you, though I expected nothing better from Charles Lomax.

CUSINS [in a remarkably gentle voice] Barbara has been trying to teach me the West Ham Salvation March.

LADY BRITOMART. I see nothing to laugh at in that; nor should you if you are really converted.

CUSINS [sweetly] You were not present. It was really funny, I believe.

LOMAX. Ripping.

LADY BRITOMART. Be quiet, Charles. Now listen to me, children. Your father is coming here this evening. [General stupefaction].

LOMAX [remonstrating] Oh I say!

LADY BRITOMART. You are not called on to say anything, Charles.

SARAH. Are you serious, mother?

LADY BRITOMART. Of course I am serious. It is on your account, Sarah, and also on Charles's. [Silence. Charles looks painfully unworthy]. I hope you are not going to object, Barbara.

BARBARA. I! why should I? My father has a soul to be saved like anybody else. He's quite welcome as far as I am concerned.

LOMAX [still remonstrant] But really, don't you know! Oh I say!

LADY BRITOMART [frigidly] What do you wish to convey, Charles?

LOMAX. Well, you must admit that this is a bit thick.

LADY BRITOMART [turning with ominous suavity to Cusins] Adolphus: you are a professor of Greek. Can you translate Charles Lomax's remarks into reputable English for us?

CUSINS [cautiously] If I may say so, Lady Brit, I think Charles has rather happily expressed what we all feel. Homer, speaking of Autolycus, uses the same phrase.

LOMAX [handsomely] Not that I mind, you know, if Sarah don't.

LADY BRITOMART [crushingly] Thank you. Have I your permission, Adolphus, to invite my own husband to my own house?

CUSINS [gallantly] You have my unhesitating support in everything you do.

LADY BRITOMART. Sarah: have you nothing to say?

SARAH. Do you mean that he is coming regularly to live here?

LADY BRITOMART. Certainly not. The spare room is ready for him if he likes to stay for a day or two and see a little more of you; but there are limits.

SARAH. Well, he can't eat us, I suppose. I don't mind.

LOMAX [chuckling] I wonder how the old man will take it.

LADY BRITOMART. Much as the old woman will, no doubt, Charles.

LOMAX [abashed] I didn't mean—at least—

LADY BRITOMART. You didn't think, Charles. You never do; and the result is, you never mean anything. And now please attend to me, children. Your father will be quite a stranger to us.

LOMAX. I suppose he hasn't seen Sarah since she was a little kid.

LADY BRITOMART. Not since she was a little kid, Charles, as you express it with that elegance of diction and refinement of thought that seem never to desert you. Accordingly—er— [impatiently] Now I have forgotten what I was going to say. That comes of your provoking me to be sarcastic, Charles. Adolphus: will you kindly tell me where I was.

CUSINS [sweetly] You were saying that as Mr Undershaft has not seen his children since they were babies, he will form his opinion of the way you have brought them up from their behavior to-night, and that therefore you wish us all to be particularly careful to conduct ourselves well, especially Charles.

LOMAX. Look here: Lady Brit didn't say that.

LADY BRITOMART [vehemently] I did, Charles. Adolphus's recollection is perfectly correct. It is most important that you should be good; and I do beg you for once not to pair off into opposite corners and giggle and whisper while I am speaking to your father.

BARBARA. All right, mother. We'll do you credit.

LADY BRITOMART. Remember, Charles, that Sarah will want to feel proud of you instead of ashamed of you.

LOMAX. Oh I say! There's nothing to be exactly proud of, don't you know.

LADY BRITOMART. Well, try and look as if there was.

Morrison, pale and dismayed, breaks into the room in unconcealed disorder.

MORRISON. Might I speak a word to you, my lady?

LADY BRITOMART. Nonsense! Show him up.

MORRISON. Yes, my lady. [He goes].

LOMAX. Does Morrison know who he is?

LADY BRITOMART. Of course. Morrison has always been with us.

LOMAX. It must be a regular corker for him, don't you know.

LADY BRITOMART. Is this a moment to get on my nerves, Charles, with your outrageous expressions?

LOMAX. But this is something out of the ordinary, really—

MORRISON [at the door] The—er—Mr Undershaft. [He retreats in confusion].

Andrew Undershaft comes in. All rise. Lady Britomart meets him in the middle of the room behind the settee.

Andrew is, on the surface, a stoutish, easygoing elderly man, with kindly patient manners, and an engaging simplicity of character. But he has a watchful, deliberate, waiting, listening face, and formidable reserves of power, both bodily and mental, in his capacious chest and long head. His gentleness is partly that of a strong man who has learnt by experience that his natural grip hurts ordinary people unless he handles them very carefully, and partly the mellowness of age and success. He is also a little shy in his present very delicate situation.

LADY BRITOMART. Good evening, Andrew.

UNDERSHAFT. How d'ye do, my dear.

LADY BRITOMART. You look a good deal older.

UNDERSHAFT [apologetically] I AM somewhat older. [With a touch of courtship] Time has stood still with you.

LADY BRITOMART [promptly] Rubbish! This is your family.

UNDERSHAFT [surprised] Is it so large? I am sorry to say my memory is failing very badly in some things. [He offers his hand with paternal kindness to Lomax].

LOMAX [jerkily shaking his hand] Ahdedoo.

UNDERSHAFT. I can see you are my eldest. I am very glad to meet you again, my boy.

LOMAX [remonstrating] No but look here don't you know—[Overcome] Oh I say!

LADY BRITOMART [recovering from momentary speechlessness] Andrew: do you mean to say that you don't remember how many children you have?

UNDERSHAFT. Well, I am afraid I—. They have grown so much—er. Am I making any ridiculous mistake? I may as well confess: I recollect only one son. But so many things have happened since, of course—er—

LADY BRITOMART [decisively] Andrew: you are talking nonsense. Of course you have only one son.

UNDERSHAFT. Perhaps you will be good enough to introduce me, my dear.

LADY BRITOMART. That is Charles Lomax, who is engaged to Sarah.

UNDERSHAFT. My dear sir, I beg your pardon.

LOMAX. Not at all. Delighted, I assure you.

LADY BRITOMART. This is Stephen.

UNDERSHAFT [bowing] Happy to make your acquaintance, Mr Stephen. Then [going to Cusins] you must be my son. [Taking Cusins' hands in his] How are you, my young friend? [To Lady Britomart] He is very like you, my love.

CUSINS. You flatter me, Mr Undershaft. My name is Cusins: engaged to Barbara. [Very explicitly] That is Major Barbara Undershaft, of the Salvation Army. That is Sarah, your second daughter. This is Stephen Undershaft, your son.

UNDERSHAFT. My dear Stephen, I beg your pardon.

STEPHEN. Not at all.

UNDERSHAFT. Mr Cusins: I am much indebted to you for explaining so precisely. [Turning to Sarah] Barbara, my dear—

SARAH [prompting him] Sarah.

UNDERSHAFT. Sarah, of course. [They shake hands. He goes over to Barbara] Barbara—I am right this time, I hope.

BARBARA. Quite right. [They shake hands].

LADY BRITOMART [resuming command] Sit down, all of you. Sit down, Andrew. [She comes forward and sits on the settle. Cusins also brings his chair forward on her left. Barbara and Stephen resume their seats. Lomax gives his chair to Sarah and goes for another].

UNDERSHAFT. Thank you, my love.

LOMAX [conversationally, as he brings a chair forward between the writing table and the settee, and offers it to Undershaft] Takes you some time to find out exactly where you are, don't it?

UNDERSHAFT [accepting the chair] That is not what embarrasses me, Mr

Lomax. My difficulty is that if I play the part of a father, I shall produce the effect of an intrusive stranger; and if I play the part of a discreet stranger, I may appear a callous father.

LADY BRITOMART. There is no need for you to play any part at all, Andrew. You had much better be sincere and natural.

UNDERSHAFT [submissively] Yes, my dear: I daresay that will be best. [Making himself comfortable] Well, here I am. Now what can I do for you all?

LADY BRITOMART. You need not do anything, Andrew. You are one of the family. You can sit with us and enjoy yourself.

Lomax's too long suppressed mirth explodes in agonized neighings.

LADY BRITOMART [outraged] Charles Lomax: if you can behave yourself, behave yourself. If not, leave the room.

LOMAX. I'm awfully sorry, Lady Brit; but really, you know, upon my soul! [He sits on the settee between Lady Britomart and Undershaft, quite overcome].

BARBARA. Why don't you laugh if you want to, Cholly? It's good for your inside.

LADY BRITOMART. Barbara: you have had the education of a lady. Please let your father see that; and don't talk like a street girl.

UNDERSHAFT. Never mind me, my dear. As you know, I am not a gentleman; and I was never educated.

LOMAX [encouragingly] Nobody'd know it, I assure you. You look all right, you know.

CUSINS. Let me advise you to study Greek, Mr Undershaft. Greek scholars are privileged men. Few of them know Greek; and none of them know anything else; but their position is unchallengeable. Other languages are the qualifications of waiters and commercial travellers: Greek is to a man of position what the hallmark is to silver.

BARBARA. Dolly: don't be insincere. Cholly: fetch your concertina and play something for us.

LOMAX [doubtfully to Undershaft] Perhaps that sort of thing isn't in your line, eh?

UNDERSHAFT. I am particularly fond of music.

LOMAX [delighted] Are you? Then I'll get it. [He goes upstairs for the instrument].

UNDERSHAFT. Do you play, Barbara?

BARBARA. Only the tambourine. But Cholly's teaching me the concertina.

UNDERSHAFT. Is Cholly also a member of the Salvation Army?

BARBARA. No: he says it's bad form to be a dissenter. But I don't despair of Cholly. I made him come yesterday to a meeting at the dock gates, and take the collection in his hat.

LADY BRITOMART. It is not my doing, Andrew. Barbara is old enough to take her own way. She has no father to advise her.

BARBARA. Oh yes she has. There are no orphans in the Salvation Army.

UNDERSHAFT. Your father there has a great many children and plenty of experience, eh?

BARBARA [looking at him with quick interest and nodding] Just so. How did you come to understand that? [Lomax is heard at the door trying the concertina].

LADY BRITOMART. Come in, Charles. Play us something at once.

LOMAX. Righto! [He sits down in his former place, and preludes].

UNDERSHAFT. One moment, Mr Lomax. I am rather interested in the Salvation Army. Its motto might be my own: Blood and Fire.

LOMAX [shocked] But not your sort of blood and fire, you know.

UNDERSHAFT. My sort of blood cleanses: my sort of fire purifies.

BARBARA. So do ours. Come down to-morrow to my shelter—the West Ham shelter—and see what we're doing. We're going to march to a great meeting in the Assembly Hall at Mile End. Come and see the shelter and then march with us: it will do you a lot of good. Can you play anything?

UNDERSHAFT. In my youth I earned pennies, and even shillings occasionally, in the streets and in public house parlors by my natural talent for stepdancing. Later on, I became a member of the Undershaft orchestral society, and performed passably on the tenor trombone.

LOMAX [scandalized] Oh I say!

BARBARA. Many a sinner has played himself into heaven on the trombone, thanks to the Army.

LOMAX [to Barbara, still rather shocked] Yes; but what about the cannon business, don't you know? [To Undershaft] Getting into heaven is not exactly in your line, is it?

LADY BRITOMART. Charles!!!

LOMAX. Well; but it stands to reason, don't it? The cannon business may be necessary and all that: we can't get on without cannons; but it isn't right, you know. On the other hand, there may be a certain amount of tosh about the Salvation Army—I belong to the Established Church myself—but still you can't deny that it's religion; and you can't go against religion, can you? At least unless you're downright immoral, don't you know.

UNDERSHAFT. You hardly appreciate my position, Mr Lomax—

LOMAX [hastily] I'm not saying anything against you personally, you know.

UNDERSHAFT. Quite so, quite so. But consider for a moment. Here I am, a manufacturer of mutilation and murder. I find myself in a specially amiable humor just now because, this morning, down at the foundry, we blew twenty-seven dummy soldiers into fragments with a gun which formerly destroyed only thirteen.

LOMAX [leniently] Well, the more destructive war becomes, the sooner it will be abolished, eh?

UNDERSHAFT. Not at all. The more destructive war becomes the more fascinating we find it. No, Mr Lomax, I am obliged to you for making the usual excuse for my trade; but I am not ashamed of it. I am not one of those men who keep their morals and their business in watertight compartments. All the spare money my trade rivals spend on hospitals, cathedrals and other receptacles for conscience money, I devote to experiments and researches in improved methods of destroying life and property. I have always done so; and I always shall. Therefore your Christmas card moralities of peace on earth and goodwill among men are of no use to me. Your Christianity, which enjoins you to resist not evil, and to turn the other cheek, would make me a bankrupt. My morality—my religion—must have a place for cannons and torpedoes in it.

STEPHEN [coldly—almost sullenly] You speak as if there were half a dozen moralities and religions to choose from, instead of one true morality and one true religion.

UNDERSHAFT. For me there is only one true morality; but it might not fit you, as you do not manufacture aerial battleships. There is only one true morality for every man; but every man has not the same true morality.

LOMAX [overtaxed] Would you mind saying that again? I didn't quite follow it.

CUSINS. It's quite simple. As Euripides says, one man's meat is another man's poison morally as well as physically.

UNDERSHAFT. Precisely.

LOMAX. Oh, that. Yes, yes, yes. True. True.

STEPHEN. In other words, some men are honest and some are scoundrels.

BARBARA. Bosh. There are no scoundrels.

UNDERSHAFT. Indeed? Are there any good men?

BARBARA. No. Not one. There are neither good men nor scoundrels: there are just children of one Father; and the sooner they stop calling one another names the better. You needn't talk to me: I know them. I've had scores of them through my hands: scoundrels, criminals, infidels, philanthropists, missionaries, county councillors, all sorts. They're all just the same sort of sinner; and there's the same salvation ready for them all.

UNDERSHAFT. May I ask have you ever saved a maker of cannons?

BARBARA. No. Will you let me try?

UNDERSHAFT. Well, I will make a bargain with you. If I go to see you to-morrow in your Salvation Shelter, will you come the day after to see me in my cannon works?

BARBARA. Take care. It may end in your giving up the cannons for the sake of the Salvation Army.

UNDERSHAFT. Are you sure it will not end in your giving up the Salvation Army for the sake of the cannons?

BARBARA. I will take my chance of that.

UNDERSHAFT. And I will take my chance of the other. [They shake hands on it]. Where is your shelter?

BARBARA. In West Ham. At the sign of the cross. Ask anybody in Canning Town. Where are your works?

UNDERSHAFT. In Perivale St Andrews. At the sign of the sword. Ask anybody in Europe.

LOMAX. Hadn't I better play something?

BARBARA. Yes. Give us Onward, Christian Soldiers.

LOMAX. Well, that's rather a strong order to begin with, don't you know. Suppose I sing Thou'rt passing hence, my brother. It's much the same tune.

BARBARA. It's too melancholy. You get saved, Cholly; and you'll pass hence, my brother, without making such a fuss about it.

LADY BRITOMART. Really, Barbara, you go on as if religion were a pleasant subject. Do have some sense of propriety.

UNDERSHAFT. I do not find it an unpleasant subject, my dear. It is the only one that capable people really care for.

LADY BRITOMART [looking at her watch] Well, if you are determined to have it, I insist on having it in a proper and respectable way. Charles: ring for prayers. [General amazement. Stephen rises in dismay].

LOMAX [rising] Oh I say!

UNDERSHAFT [rising] I am afraid I must be going.

LADY BRITOMART. You cannot go now, Andrew: it would be most improper. Sit down. What will the servants think?

UNDERSHAFT. My dear: I have conscientious scruples. May I suggest a compromise? If Barbara will conduct a little service in the drawingroom, with Mr Lomax as organist, I will attend it willingly. I will even take part, if a trombone can be procured.

LADY BRITOMART. Don't mock, Andrew.

UNDERSHAFT [shocked—to Barbara] You don't think I am mocking, my love, I hope.

BARBARA. No, of course not; and it wouldn't matter if you were: half the Army came to their first meeting for a lark. [Rising] Come along. Come, Dolly. Come, Cholly. [She goes out with Undershaft, who opens the door for her. Cusins rises].

LADY BRITOMART. I will not be disobeyed by everybody. Adolphus: sit down. Charles: you may go. You are not fit for prayers: you cannot keep your countenance.

LOMAX. Oh I say! [He goes out].

LADY BRITOMART [continuing] But you, Adolphus, can behave yourself if you choose to. I insist on your staying.

CUSINS. My dear Lady Brit: there are things in the family prayer book that I couldn't bear to hear you say.

LADY BRITOMART. What things, pray?

CUSINS. Well, you would have to say before all the servants that we have done things we ought not to have done, and left undone things we ought to have done, and that there is no health in us. I cannot bear to hear you doing yourself such an unjustice, and Barbara such an injustice. As for myself, I flatly deny it: I have done my best. I shouldn't dare to marry Barbara—I couldn't look you in the face—if it were true. So I must go to the drawingroom.

LADY BRITOMART [offended] Well, go. [He starts for the door]. And remember this, Adolphus [he turns to listen]: I have a very strong suspicion that you went to the Salvation Army to worship Barbara and nothing else. And I quite appreciate the very clever way in which you systematically humbug me. I have found you out. Take care Barbara doesn't. That's all.

CUSINS [with unruffled sweetness] Don't tell on me. [He goes out].

LADY BRITOMART. Sarah: if you want to go, go. Anything's better than to sit there as if you wished you were a thousand miles away.

SARAH [languidly] Very well, mamma. [She goes].

Lady Britomart, with a sudden flounce, gives way to a little gust of tears.

STEPHEN [going to her] Mother: what's the matter?

LADY BRITOMART [swishing away her tears with her handkerchief] Nothing. Foolishness. You can go with him, too, if you like, and leave me with the servants.

STEPHEN. Oh, you mustn't think that, mother. I—I don't like him.

LADY BRITOMART. The others do. That is the injustice of a woman's lot. A woman has to bring up her children; and that means to restrain them, to deny them things they want, to set them tasks, to punish them when they do wrong, to do all the unpleasant things. And then the father, who has nothing to do but pet them and spoil them, comes in when all her work is done and steals their affection from her.

STEPHEN. He has not stolen our affection from you. It is only curiosity.

LADY BRITOMART [violently] I won't be consoled, Stephen. There is nothing the matter with me. [She rises and goes towards the door].

STEPHEN. Where are you going, mother?

LADY BRITOMART. To the drawingroom, of course. [She goes out. Onward, Christian Soldiers, on the concertina, with tambourine accompaniment, is heard when the door opens]. Are you coming, Stephen?

STEPHEN. No. Certainly not. [She goes. He sits down on the settee, with compressed lips and an expression of strong dislike].

ACT II

The yard of the West Ham shelter of the Salvation Army is a cold place on a January morning. The building itself, an old warehouse, is newly whitewashed. Its gabled end projects into the yard in the middle, with a door on the ground floor, and another in the loft above it without any balcony or ladder, but with a pulley rigged over it for hoisting sacks. Those who come from this central gable end into the yard have the gateway leading to the street on their left, with a stone horse-trough just beyond it, and, on the right, a penthouse shielding a table from the weather. There are forms at the table; and on them are seated a man and a woman, both much down on their luck, finishing a meal of bread [one thick slice each, with margarine and golden syrup] and diluted milk.

The man, a workman out of employment, is young, agile, a talker, a poser, sharp enough to be capable of anything in reason except honesty or altruistic considerations of any kind. The woman is a commonplace old bundle of poverty and hard-worn humanity. She looks sixty and probably is forty-five. If they were rich people, gloved and muffed and well wrapped up in furs and overcoats, they would be numbed and miserable; for it is a grindingly cold, raw, January day; and a glance at the background of grimy warehouses and leaden sky visible over the whitewashed walls of the yard would drive any idle rich person straight to the Mediterranean. But these two, being no more troubled with visions of the Mediterranean than of the moon, and being compelled to keep more of their clothes in the pawnshop, and less on their persons, in winter than in summer, are not depressed by the cold: rather are they stung into vivacity, to which their meal has just now given an almost jolly turn. The man takes a pull at his mug, and then gets up and moves about the yard with his hands deep in his pockets, occasionally breaking into a step-dance.

THE WOMAN. Feel better otter your meal, sir?

THE MAN. No. Call that a meal! Good enough for you, props; but wot is it to me, an intelligent workin man.

THE WOMAN. Workin man! Wot are you?

THE MAN. Painter.

THE WOMAN [sceptically] Yus, I dessay.

THE MAN. Yus, you dessay! I know. Every loafer that can't do nothink calls isself a painter. Well, I'm a real painter: grainer, finisher, thirty-eight bob a week when I can get it.

THE WOMAN. Then why don't you go and get it?

THE MAN. I'll tell you why. Fust: I'm intelligent—fffff! it's rotten cold here [he dances a step or two]—yes: intelligent beyond the station o life into which it has pleased the capitalists to call me; and they don't like a man that sees through em. Second, an intelligent bein needs a doo share of appiness; so I drink somethink cruel when I get the chawnce. Third, I stand by my class and do as little as I can so's to leave arf the job for me fellow workers. Fourth, I'm fly enough to know wots inside the law and wots outside it; and inside it I do as the capitalists do: pinch wot I can lay me ands on. In a proper state of society I am sober, industrious and honest: in Rome, so to speak, I do as the Romans do. Wots the consequence? When trade is bad—and it's rotten bad just now—and the employers az to sack arf their men, they generally start on me.

THE WOMAN. What's your name?

THE MAN. Price. Bronterre O'Brien Price. Usually called Snobby Price, for short.

THE WOMAN. Snobby's a carpenter, ain't it? You said you was a painter.

PRICE. Not that kind of snob, but the genteel sort. I'm too uppish, owing to my intelligence, and my father being a Chartist and a reading, thinking man: a stationer, too. I'm none of your common hewers of wood and drawers of water; and don't you forget it. [He returns to his seat at the table, and takes up his mug]. Wots YOUR name?

THE WOMAN. Rummy Mitchens, sir.

PRICE [quaffing the remains of his milk to her] Your elth, Miss Mitchens.

RUMMY [correcting him] Missis Mitchens.

PRICE. Wot! Oh Rummy, Rummy! Respectable married woman, Rummy, gittin rescued by the Salvation Army by pretendin to be a bad un. Same old game!

RUMMY. What am I to do? I can't starve. Them Salvation lasses is dear good girls; but the better you are, the worse they likes to think you were before they rescued you. Why shouldn't they av a bit o credit, poor loves? They're worn to rags by their work. And where would they get the money to rescue us if we was to let on we're no worse than other people? You know what ladies and gentlemen are.

PRICE. Thievin swine! Wish I ad their job, Rummy, all the same. Wot does Rummy stand for? Pet name props?

RUMMY. Short for Romola.

PRICE. For wot!?

RUMMY. Romola. It was out of a new book. Somebody me mother wanted me to grow up like.

PRICE. We're companions in misfortune, Rummy. Both on us got names that nobody cawnt pronounce. Consequently I'm Snobby and you're Rummy because Bill and Sally wasn't good enough for our parents. Such is life!

RUMMY. Who saved you, Mr. Price? Was it Major Barbara?

PRICE. No: I come here on my own. I'm goin to be Bronterre O'Brien Price, the converted painter. I know wot they like. I'll tell em how I blasphemed and gambled and wopped my poor old mother—

RUMMY [shocked] Used you to beat your mother?

PRICE. Not likely. She used to beat me. No matter: you come and listen to the converted painter, and you'll hear how she was a pious woman that taught me me prayers at er knee, an how I used to come home drunk and drag her out o bed be er snow white airs, an lam into er with the poker.

RUMMY. That's what's so unfair to us women. Your confessions is just as big lies as ours: you don't tell what you really done no more than us; but you men can tell your lies right out at the meetins and be made much of for it; while the sort o confessions we az to make az to be wispered to one lady at a time. It ain't right, spite of all their piety.

PRICE. Right! Do you spose the Army'd be allowed if it went and did right? Not much. It combs our air and makes us good little blokes to be robbed and put upon. But I'll play the game as good as any of em. I'll see somebody struck by lightnin, or hear a voice sayin "Snobby Price: where will you spend eternity?" I'll ave a time of it, I tell you.

RUMMY. You won't be let drink, though.

PRICE. I'll take it out in gorspellin, then. I don't want to drink if I can get fun enough any other way.

Jenny Hill, a pale, overwrought, pretty Salvation lass of 18, comes in through the yard gate, leading Peter Shirley, a half hardened, half worn-out elderly man, weak with hunger.

JENNY [supporting him] Come! pluck up. I'll get you something to eat. You'll be all right then.

PRICE [rising and hurrying officiously to take the old man off Jenny's hands] Poor old man! Cheer up, brother: you'll find rest and peace and appiness ere. Hurry up with the food, miss: e's fair done. [Jenny hurries into the shelter]. Ere, buck up, daddy! She's fetchin y'a thick slice o breadn treacle, an a mug o skyblue. [He seats him at the corner of the table].

RUMMY [gaily] Keep up your old art! Never say die!

SHIRLEY. I'm not an old man. I'm ony 46. I'm as good as ever I was. The grey patch come in my hair before I was thirty. All it wants is three pennorth o hair dye: am I to be turned on the streets to starve for it? Holy God! I've worked ten to twelve hours a day since I was thirteen, and paid my way all through; and now am I to be thrown into the gutter and my job given to a young man that can do it no better than me because I've black hair that goes white at the first change?

PRICE [cheerfully] No good jawrin about it. You're ony a jumped-up, jerked-off, orspittle-turned-out incurable of an ole workin man: who cares about you? Eh? Make the thievin swine give you a meal: they've stole many a one from you. Get a bit o your own back. [Jenny returns with the usual meal]. There you are, brother. Awsk a blessin an tuck that into you.

SHIRLEY [looking at it ravenously but not touching it, and crying like a child] I never took anything before.

JENNY [petting him] Come, come! the Lord sends it to you: he wasn't above taking bread from his friends; and why should you be? Besides, when we find you a job you can pay us for it if you like.

SHIRLEY [eagerly] Yes, yes: that's true. I can pay you back: it's only a loan. [Shivering] Oh Lord! oh Lord! [He turns to the table and attacks the meal ravenously].

JENNY. Well, Rummy, are you more comfortable now?

RUMMY. God bless you, lovey! You've fed my body and saved my soul, haven't you? [Jenny, touched, kisses her] Sit down and rest a bit: you must be ready to drop.

JENNY. I've been going hard since morning. But there's more work than we can do. I mustn't stop.

RUMMY. Try a prayer for just two minutes. You'll work all the better after.

JENNY [her eyes lighting up] Oh isn't it wonderful how a few minutes prayer revives you! I was quite lightheaded at twelve o'clock, I was so tired; but Major Barbara just sent me to pray for five minutes; and I was able to go on as if I had only just begun. [To Price] Did you have a piece of bread?

PAIGE [with unction] Yes, miss; but I've got the piece that I value more; and that's the peace that passeth hall hannerstennin.

RUMMY [fervently] Glory Hallelujah!

Bill Walker, a rough customer of about 25, appears at the yard gate and looks malevolently at Jenny.

JENNY. That makes me so happy. When you say that, I feel wicked for loitering here. I must get to work again.

She is hurrying to the shelter, when the new-comer moves quickly up to the door and intercepts her. His manner is so threatening that she retreats as he comes at her truculently, driving her down the yard.

BILL. I know you. You're the one that took away my girl. You're the one that set er agen me. Well, I'm goin to av er out. Not that I care a curse for her or you: see? But I'll let er know; and I'll let you know. I'm goin to give er a doin that'll teach er to cut away from me. Now in with you and tell er to come out afore I come in and kick er out. Tell er Bill Walker wants er. She'll know what that means; and if she keeps me waitin it'll be worse. You stop to jaw back at me; and I'll start on you: d'ye hear? There's your way. In you go. [He takes her by the arm and slings her towards the door of the shelter. She falls on her hand and knee. Rummy helps her up again].

PRICE [rising, and venturing irresolutely towards Bill]. Easy there, mate. She ain't doin you no arm.

BILL. Who are you callin mate? [Standing over him threateningly]. You're goin to stand up for her, are you? Put up your ands.

RUMMY [running indignantly to him to scold him]. Oh, you great brute— [He instantly swings his left hand back against her face. She screams and reels back to the trough, where she sits down, covering her bruised face with her hands and rocking and moaning with pain].

JENNY [going to her]. Oh God forgive you! How could you strike an old woman like that?

BILL [seizing her by the hair so violently that she also screams, and tearing her away from the old woman]. You Gawd forgive me again and I'll Gawd forgive you one on the jaw that'll stop you prayin for a week.

[Holding her and turning fiercely on Price]. Av you anything to say agen it? Eh?

PRICE [intimidated]. No, matey: she ain't anything to do with me.

BILL. Good job for you! I'd put two meals into you and fight you with one finger after, you starved cur. [To Jenny] Now are you goin to fetch out Mog Habbijam; or am I to knock your face off you and fetch her myself?

JENNY [writhing in his grasp] Oh please someone go in and tell Major Barbara—[she screams again as he wrenches her head down; and Price and Rummy, flee into the shelter].

BILL. You want to go in and tell your Major of me, do you?

JENNY. Oh please don't drag my hair. Let me go.

BILL. Do you or don't you? [She stifles a scream]. Yes or no.

JENNY. God give me strength—

BILL [striking her with his fist in the face] Go and show her that, and tell her if she wants one like it to come and interfere with me. [Jenny, crying with pain, goes into the shed. He goes to the form and addresses the old man]. Here: finish your mess; and get out o my way.

SHIRLEY [springing up and facing him fiercely, with the mug in his hand] You take a liberty with me, and I'll smash you over the face with the mug and cut your eye out. Ain't you satisfied—young whelps like you—with takin the bread out o the mouths of your elders that have brought you up and slaved for you, but you must come shovin and cheekin and bullyin in here, where the bread o charity is sickenin in our stummicks?

BILL [contemptuously, but backing a little] Wot good are you, you old palsy mug? Wot good are you?

SHIRLEY. As good as you and better. I'll do a day's work agen you or any fat young soaker of your age. Go and take my job at Horrockses, where I worked for ten year. They want young men there: they can't afford to keep men over forty-five. They're very sorry—give you a character and happy to help you to get anything suited to your years—sure a steady man won't be long out of a job. Well, let em try you. They'll find the differ. What do you know? Not as much as how to beeyave yourself—layin your dirty fist across the mouth of a respectable woman!

BILL. Don't provoke me to lay it acrost yours: d'ye hear?

SHIRLEY [with blighting contempt] Yes: you like an old man to hit, don't you, when you've finished with the women. I ain't seen you hit a young one yet.

BILL [stung] You lie, you old soupkitchener, you. There was a young man here. Did I offer to hit him or did I not?

SHIRLEY. Was he starvin or was he not? Was he a man or only a crosseyed thief an a loafer? Would you hit my son-in-law's brother?

BILL. Who's he?

SHIRLEY. Todger Fairmile o Balls Pond. Him that won 20 pounds off the Japanese wrastler at the music hall by standin out 17 minutes 4 seconds agen him.

BILL [sullenly] I'm no music hall wrastler. Can he box?

SHIRLEY. Yes: an you can't.

BILL. Wot! I can't, can't I? Wot's that you say [threatening him]?

SHIRLEY [not budging an inch] Will you box Todger Fairmile if I put him on to you? Say the word.

BILL. [subsiding with a slouch] I'll stand up to any man alive, if he was ten Todger Fairmiles. But I don't set up to be a perfessional.

SHIRLEY [looking down on him with unfathomable disdain] YOU box! Slap an old woman with the back o your hand! You hadn't even the sense to hit her where a magistrate couldn't see the mark of it, you silly young lump of conceit and ignorance. Hit a girl in the jaw and ony make her cry! If Todger Fairmile'd done it, she wouldn't a got up inside o ten minutes, no more than you would if he got on to you. Yah! I'd set about you myself if I had a week's feedin in me instead o two months starvation. [He returns to the table to finish his meal].

BILL [following him and stooping over him to drive the taunt in] You lie! you have the bread and treacle in you that you come here to beg.

SHIRLEY [bursting into tears] Oh God! it's true: I'm only an old pauper on the scrap heap. [Furiously] But you'll come to it yourself; and then you'll know. You'll come to it sooner than a teetotaller like me, fillin yourself with gin at this hour o the mornin!

BILL. I'm no gin drinker, you old liar; but when I want to give my girl a bloomin good idin I like to av a bit o devil in me: see? An here I am, talkin to a rotten old blighter like you sted o givin her wot for. [Working himself into a rage] I'm goin in there to fetch her out. [He makes vengefully for the shelter door].

SHIRLEY. You're goin to the station on a stretcher, more likely; and they'll take the gin and the devil out of you there when they get you inside. You mind what you're about: the major here is the Earl o Stevenage's granddaughter.

BILL [checked] Garn!

SHIRLEY. You'll see.

BILL [his resolution oozing] Well, I ain't done nothin to er.

SHIRLEY. Spose she said you did! who'd believe you?

BILL [very uneasy, skulking back to the corner of the penthouse] Gawd! There's no jastice in this country. To think wot them people can do! I'm as good as er.

SHIRLEY. Tell her so. It's just what a fool like you would do.

Barbara, brisk and businesslike, comes from the shelter with a note book, and addresses herself to Shirley. Bill, cowed, sits down in the corner on a form, and turns his back on them.

BARBARA. Good morning.

SHIRLEY [standing up and taking off his hat] Good morning, miss.

BARBARA. Sit down: make yourself at home. [He hesitates; but she puts a friendly hand on his shoulder and makes him obey]. Now then! since you've made friends with us, we want to know all about you. Names and addresses and trades.

SHIRLEY. Peter Shirley. Fitter. Chucked out two months ago because I was too old.

BARBARA [not at all surprised] You'd pass still. Why didn't you dye your hair?

SHIRLEY. I did. Me age come out at a coroner's inquest on me daughter.

BARBARA. Steady?

SHIRLEY. Teetotaller. Never out of a job before. Good worker. And sent to the knockers like an old horse!

BARBARA. No matter: if you did your part God will do his.

SHIRLEY [suddenly stubborn] My religion's no concern of anybody but myself.

BARBARA [guessing] I know. Secularist?

SHIRLEY [hotly] Did I offer to deny it?

BARBARA. Why should you? My own father's a Secularist, I think. Our Father—yours and mine—fulfils himself in many ways; and I daresay he knew what he was about when he made a Secularist of you. So buck up, Peter! we can always find a job for a steady man like you. [Shirley, disarmed, touches his hat. She turns from him to Bill]. What's your name?

BILL [insolently] Wot's that to you?

BARBARA [calmly making a note] Afraid to give his name. Any trade?

BILL. Who's afraid to give his name? [Doggedly, with a sense of heroically defying the House of Lords in the person of Lord Stevenage] If you want to bring a charge agen me, bring it. [She waits, unruffled]. My name's Bill Walker.

BARBARA [as if the name were familiar: trying to remember how] Bill Walker? [Recollecting] Oh, I know: you're the man that Jenny Hill was praying for inside just now. [She enters his name in her note book].

BILL. Who's Jenny Hill? And what call has she to pray for me?

BARBARA. I don't know. Perhaps it was you that cut her lip.

BILL [defiantly] Yes, it was me that cut her lip. I ain't afraid o you.

BARBARA. How could you be, since you're not afraid of God? You're a brave man, Mr. Walker. It takes some pluck to do our work here; but none of us dare lift our hand against a girl like that, for fear of her father in heaven.

BILL [sullenly] I want none o your cantin jaw. I suppose you think I come here to beg from you, like this damaged lot here. Not me. I don't want your bread and scrape and catlap. I don't believe in your Gawd, no more than you do yourself.

BARBARA [sunnily apologetic and ladylike, as on a new footing with him] Oh, I beg your pardon for putting your name down, Mr. Walker. I didn't understand. I'll strike it out.

BILL [taking this as a slight, and deeply wounded by it] Eah! you let my name alone. Ain't it good enough to be in your book?

BARBARA [considering] Well, you see, there's no use putting down your name unless I can do something for you, is there? What's your trade?

BILL [still smarting] That's no concern o yours.

BARBARA. Just so. [very businesslike] I'll put you down as [writing] the man who—struck—poor little Jenny Hill—in the mouth.

BILL [rising threateningly] See here. I've ad enough o this.

BARBARA [quite sunny and fearless] What did you come to us for?

BILL. I come for my girl, see? I come to take her out o this and to break er jaws for her.

BARBARA [complacently] You see I was right about your trade. [Bill, on the point of retorting furiously, finds himself, to his great shame and terror, in danger of crying instead. He sits down again suddenly]. What's her name?

BILL [dogged] Er name's Mog Abbijam: thats wot her name is.

BARBARA. Oh, she's gone to Canning Town, to our barracks there.

BILL [fortified by his resentment of Mog's perfidy] is she? [Vindictively] Then I'm goin to Kennintahn arter her. [He crosses to the gate; hesitates; finally comes back at Barbara]. Are you lyin to me to get shut o me?

BARBARA. I don't want to get shut of you. I want to keep you here and save your soul. You'd better stay: you're going to have a bad time today, Bill.

BILL. Who's goin to give it to me? You, props.

BARBARA. Someone you don't believe in. But you'll be glad afterwards.

BILL [slinking off] I'll go to Kennintahn to be out o the reach o your tongue. [Suddenly turning on her with intense malice] And if I don't find Mog there, I'll come back and do two years for you, selp me Gawd if I don't!

BARBARA [a shade kindlier, if possible] It's no use, Bill. She's got another bloke.

BILL. Wot!

BARBARA. One of her own converts. He fell in love with her when he saw her with her soul saved, and her face clean, and her hair washed.

BILL [surprised] Wottud she wash it for, the carroty slut? It's red.

BARBARA. It's quite lovely now, because she wears a new look in her eyes with it. It's a pity you're too late. The new bloke has put your nose out of joint, Bill.

BILL. I'll put his nose out o joint for him. Not that I care a curse for her, mind that. But I'll teach her to drop me as if I was dirt. And I'll teach him to meddle with my Judy. Wots iz bleedin name?

BARBARA. Sergeant Todger Fairmile.

SHIRLEY [rising with grim joy] I'll go with him, miss. I want to see them two meet. I'll take him to the infirmary when it's over.

BILL [to Shirley, with undissembled misgiving] Is that im you was speakin on?

SHIRLEY. That's him.

BILL. Im that wrastled in the music all?

SHIRLEY. The competitions at the National Sportin Club was worth nigh a hundred a year to him. He's gev em up now for religion; so he's a bit fresh for want of the exercise he was accustomed to. He'll be glad to see you. Come along.

BILL. Wots is weight?

SHIRLEY. Thirteen four. [Bill's last hope expires].

BARBARA. Go and talk to him, Bill. He'll convert you.

SHIRLEY. He'll convert your head into a mashed potato.

BILL [sullenly] I ain't afraid of him. I ain't afraid of ennybody. But he can lick me. She's done me. [He sits down moodily on the edge of the horse trough].

SHIRLEY. You ain't goin. I thought not. [He resumes his seat].

BARBARA [calling] Jenny!

JENNY [appearing at the shelter door with a plaster on the corner of her mouth] Yes, Major.

BARBARA. Send Rummy Mitchens out to clear away here.

JENNY. I think she's afraid.

BARBARA [her resemblance to her mother flashing out for a moment] Nonsense! she must do as she's told.

JENNY [calling into the shelter] Rummy: the Major says you must come.

Jenny comes to Barbara, purposely keeping on the side next Bill, lest he should suppose that she shrank from him or bore malice.

BARBARA. Poor little Jenny! Are you tired? [Looking at the wounded cheek] Does it hurt?

JENNY. No: it's all right now. It was nothing.

BARBARA [critically] It was as hard as he could hit, I expect. Poor Bill! You don't feel angry with him, do you?

JENNY. Oh no, no, no: indeed I don't, Major, bless his poor heart! [Barbara kisses her; and she runs away merrily into the shelter. Bill writhes with an agonizing return of his new and alarming symptoms, but says nothing. Rummy Mitchens comes from the shelter].

BARBARA [going to meet Rummy] Now Rummy, bustle. Take in those mugs and plates to be washed; and throw the crumbs about for the birds.

Rummy takes the three plates and mugs; but Shirley takes back his mug from her, as there it still come milk left in it.

RUMMY. There ain't any crumbs. This ain't a time to waste good bread on birds.

PRICE [appearing at the shelter door] Gentleman come to see the shelter, Major. Says he's your father.

BARBARA. All right. Coming. [Snobby goes back into the shelter, followed by Barbara].

RUMMY [stealing across to Bill and addressing him in a subdued voice, but with intense conviction] I'd av the lor of you, you flat eared pignosed potwalloper, if she'd let me. You're no gentleman, to hit a lady in the face. [Bill, with greater things moving in him, takes no notice].

SHIRLEY [following her] Here! in with you and don't get yourself into more trouble by talking.

RUMMY [with hauteur] I ain't ad the pleasure o being hintroduced to you, as I can remember. [She goes into the shelter with the plates].

BILL [savagely] Don't you talk to me, d'ye hear. You lea me alone, or I'll do you a mischief. I'm not dirt under your feet, anyway.

SHIRLEY [calmly] Don't you be afeerd. You ain't such prime company that you need expect to be sought after. [He is about to go into the shelter when Barbara comes out, with Undershaft on her right].

BARBARA. Oh there you are, Mr Shirley! [Between them] This is my father: I told you he was a Secularist, didn't I? Perhaps you'll be able to comfort one another.

UNDERSHAFT [startled] A Secularist! Not the least in the world: on the contrary, a confirmed mystic.

BARBARA. Sorry, I'm sure. By the way, papa, what is your religion—in case I have to introduce you again?

UNDERSHAFT. My religion? Well, my dear, I am a Millionaire. That is my religion.

BARBARA. Then I'm afraid you and Mr Shirley wont be able to comfort one another after all. You're not a Millionaire, are you, Peter?

SHIRLEY. No; and proud of it.

UNDERSHAFT [gravely] Poverty, my friend, is not a thing to be proud of.

SHIRLEY [angrily] Who made your millions for you? Me and my like. What's kep us poor? Keepin you rich. I wouldn't have your conscience, not for all your income.

UNDERSHAFT. I wouldn't have your income, not for all your conscience, Mr Shirley. [He goes to the penthouse and sits down on a form].

BARBARA [stopping Shirley adroitly as he is about to retort] You wouldn't think he was my father, would you, Peter? Will you go into the shelter and lend the lasses a hand for a while: we're worked off our feet.

SHIRLEY [bitterly] Yes: I'm in their debt for a meal, ain't I?

BARBARA. Oh, not because you're in their debt; but for love of them, Peter, for love of them. [He cannot understand, and is rather scandalized]. There! Don't stare at me. In with you; and give that conscience of yours a holiday [bustling him into the shelter].

SHIRLEY [as he goes in] Ah! it's a pity you never was trained to use your reason, miss. You'd have been a very taking lecturer on Secularism.

Barbara turns to her father.

UNDERSHAFT. Never mind me, my dear. Go about your work; and let me watch it for a while.

BARBARA. All right.

UNDERSHAFT. For instance, what's the matter with that out-patient over there?

BARBARA [looking at Bill, whose attitude has never changed, and whose expression of brooding wrath has deepened] Oh, we shall cure him in no time. Just watch. [She goes over to Bill and waits. He glances up at her and casts his eyes down again, uneasy, but grimmer than ever]. It would be nice to just stamp on Mog Habbijam's face, wouldn't it, Bill?

BILL [starting up from the trough in consternation] It's a lie: I never said so. [She shakes her head]. Who told you wot was in my mind?

BARBARA. Only your new friend.

BILL. Wot new friend?

BARBARA. The devil, Bill. When he gets round people they get miserable, just like you.

BILL [with a heartbreaking attempt at devil-may-care cheerfulness] I ain't miserable. [He sits down again, and stretches his legs in an attempt to seem indifferent].

BARBARA. Well, if you're happy, why don't you look happy, as we do?

BILL [his legs curling back in spite of him] I'm appy enough, I tell you. Why don't you lea me alown? Wot av I done to you? I ain't smashed your face, av I?

BARBARA [softly: wooing his soul] It's not me that's getting at you, Bill.

BILL. Who else is it?

BARBARA. Somebody that doesn't intend you to smash women's faces, I suppose. Somebody or something that wants to make a man of you.

BILL [blustering] Make a man o ME! Ain't I a man? eh? ain't I a man? Who sez I'm not a man?

BARBARA. There's a man in you somewhere, I suppose. But why did he let you hit poor little Jenny Hill? That wasn't very manly of him, was it?

BILL [tormented] Av done with it, I tell you. Chock it. I'm sick of your Jenny Ill and er silly little face.

BARBARA. Then why do you keep thinking about it? Why does it keep coming up against you in your mind? You're not getting converted, are you?

BILL [with conviction] Not ME. Not likely. Not arf.

BARBARA. That's right, Bill. Hold out against it. Put out your strength. Don't let's get you cheap. Todger Fairmile said he wrestled for three nights against his Salvation harder than he ever wrestled with the Jap at the music hall. He gave in to the Jap when his arm was going to break. But he didn't give in to his salvation until his heart was going to break. Perhaps you'll escape that. You haven't any heart, have you?

BILL. Wot d'ye mean? Wy ain't I got a art the same as ennybody else?

BARBARA. A man with a heart wouldn't have bashed poor little Jenny's face, would he?

BILL [almost crying] Ow, will you lea me alown? Av I ever offered to meddle with you, that you come noggin and provowkin me lawk this? [He writhes convulsively from his eyes to his toes].

BARBARA [with a steady soothing hand on his arm and a gentle voice that never lets him go] It's your soul that's hurting you, Bill, and not me. We've been through it all ourselves. Come with us, Bill. [He looks wildly round]. To brave manhood on earth and eternal glory in heaven. [He is on the point of breaking down]. Come. [A drum is heard in the shelter; and Bill, with a gasp, escapes from the spell as Barbara turns quickly. Adolphus enters from the shelter with a big drum]. Oh! there you are, Dolly. Let me introduce a new friend of mine, Mr Bill Walker. This is my bloke, Bill: Mr Cusins. [Cusins salutes with his drumstick].

BILL. Goin to marry im?

BARBARA. Yes.

BILL [fervently] Gawd elp im! Gawd elp im!

BARBARA. Why? Do you think he won't be happy with me?

BILL. I've only ad to stand it for a mornin: e'll av to stand it for a lifetime.

CUSINS. That is a frightful reflection, Mr Walker. But I can't tear myself away from her.

BILL. Well, I can. [To Barbara] Eah! do you know where I'm goin to, and wot I'm goin to do?

BARBARA. Yes: you're going to heaven; and you're coming back here before the week's out to tell me so.

BILL. You lie. I'm goin to Kennintahn, to spit in Todger Fairmile's eye. I bashed Jenny Ill's face; and now I'll get me own face bashed and come back and show it to er. E'll it me ardern I it er. That'll make us square. [To Adolphus] Is that fair or is it not? You're a genlmn: you oughter know.

BARBARA. Two black eyes wont make one white one, Bill.

BILL. I didn't ast you. Cawn't you never keep your mahth shut? I ast the genlmn.

CUSINS [reflectively] Yes: I think you're right, Mr Walker. Yes: I should do it. It's curious: it's exactly what an ancient Greek would have done.

BARBARA. But what good will it do?

CUSINS. Well, it will give Mr Fairmile some exercise; and it will satisfy Mr Walker's soul.

BILL. Rot! there ain't no sach a thing as a soul. Ah kin you tell wether I've a soul or not? You never seen it.

BARBARA. I've seen it hurting you when you went against it.

BILL [with compressed aggravation] If you was my girl and took the word out o me mahth lawk thet, I'd give you suthink you'd feel urtin, so I would. [To Adolphus] You take my tip, mate. Stop er jawr; or you'll die afore your time. [With intense expression] Wore aht: thets wot you'll be: wore aht. [He goes away through the gate].

CUSINS [looking after him] I wonder!

BARBARA. Dolly! [indignant, in her mother's manner].

CUSINS. Yes, my dear, it's very wearing to be in love with you. If it lasts, I quite think I shall die young.

BARBARA. Should you mind?

CUSINS. Not at all. [He is suddenly softened, and kisses her over the drum, evidently not for the first time, as people cannot kiss over a big drum without practice. Undershaft coughs].

BARBARA. It's all right, papa, we've not forgotten you. Dolly: explain the place to papa: I haven't time. [She goes busily into the shelter].

Undershaft and Adolpbus now have the yard to themselves. Undershaft, seated on a form, and still keenly attentive, looks hard at Adolphus. Adolphus looks hard at him.

UNDERSHAFT. I fancy you guess something of what is in my mind, Mr Cusins. [Cusins flourishes his drumsticks as if in the art of beating a lively rataplan, but makes no sound]. Exactly so. But suppose Barbara finds you out!

CUSINS. You know, I do not admit that I am imposing on Barbara. I am quite genuinely interested in the views of the Salvation Army. The fact is, I am a sort of collector of religions; and the curious thing is that I find I can believe them all. By the way, have you any religion?

UNDERSHAFT. Yes.

CUSINS. Anything out of the common?

UNDERSHAFT. Only that there are two things necessary to Salvation.

CUSINS [disappointed, but polite] Ah, the Church Catechism. Charles Lomax also belongs to the Established Church.

UNDERSHAFT. The two things are—

CUSINS. Baptism and—

UNDERSHAFT. No. Money and gunpowder.

CUSINS [surprised, but interested] That is the general opinion of our governing classes. The novelty is in hearing any man confess it.

UNDERSHAFT. Just so.

CUSINS. Excuse me: is there any place in your religion for honor, justice, truth, love, mercy and so forth?

UNDERSHAFT. Yes: they are the graces and luxuries of a rich, strong, and safe life.

CUSINS. Suppose one is forced to choose between them and money or gunpowder?

UNDERSHAFT. Choose money and gunpowder; for without enough of both you cannot afford the others.

CUSINS. That is your religion?

UNDERSHAFT. Yes.

The cadence of this reply makes a full close in the conversation. Cusins twists his face dubiously and contemplates Undershaft. Undershaft contemplates him.

CUSINS. Barbara won't stand that. You will have to choose between your religion and Barbara.

UNDERSHAFT. So will you, my friend. She will find out that that drum of yours is hollow.

CUSINS. Father Undershaft: you are mistaken: I am a sincere Salvationist. You do not understand the Salvation Army. It is the army of joy, of love, of courage: it has banished the fear and remorse and despair of the old hellridden evangelical sects: it marches to fight the devil with trumpet and drum, with music and dancing, with banner and palm, as becomes a sally from heaven by its happy garrison. It picks the waster out of the public house and makes a man of him: it finds a worm wriggling in a back kitchen, and lo! a woman! Men and women of rank too, sons and daughters of the Highest. It takes the poor professor of Greek, the most artificial and self-suppressed of human creatures, from his meal of roots, and lets loose the rhapsodist in him; reveals the true worship of Dionysos to him; sends him down the public street drumming dithyrambs [he plays a thundering flourish on the drum].

UNDERSHAFT. You will alarm the shelter.

CUSINS. Oh, they are accustomed to these sudden ecstasies of piety. However, if the drum worries you— [he pockets the drumsticks; unhooks the drum; and stands it on the ground opposite the gateway].

UNDERSHAFT. Thank you.

CUSINS. You remember what Euripides says about your money and gunpowder?

UNDERSHAFT. No.

CUSINS [declaiming]

One and another
In money and guns may outpass his brother;
And men in their millions float and flow
And seethe with a million hopes as leaven;
And they win their will; or they miss their will;
And their hopes are dead or are pined for still:
But whoe'er can know
As the long days go
That to live is happy, has found his heaven.

My translation: what do you think of it?

UNDERSHAFT. I think, my friend, that if you wish to know, as the long days go, that to live is happy, you must first acquire money enough for a decent life, and power enough to be your own master.

CUSINS. You are damnably discouraging. [He resumes his declamation].

Is it so hard a thing to see
That the spirit of God—whate'er it be—
The Law that abides and changes not, ages long,
The Eternal and Nature-born: these things be strong.
What else is Wisdom? What of Man's endeavor,
Or God's high grace so lovely and so great?
To stand from fear set free? to breathe and wait?
To hold a hand uplifted over Fate?
And shall not Barbara be loved for ever?

UNDERSHAFT. Euripides mentions Barbara, does he?

CUSINS. It is a fair translation. The word means Loveliness.

UNDERSHAFT. May I ask—as Barbara's father—how much a year she is to be loved for ever on?

CUSINS. As Barbara's father, that is more your affair than mine. I can feed her by teaching Greek: that is about all.

UNDERSHAFT. Do you consider it a good match for her?

CUSINS [with polite obstinacy] Mr Undershaft: I am in many ways a weak, timid, ineffectual person; and my health is far from satisfactory. But whenever I feel that I must have anything, I get it, sooner or later. I feel that way about Barbara. I don't like marriage: I feel intensely afraid of it; and I don't know what I shall do with Barbara or what she will do with me. But I feel that I and nobody else must marry her. Please regard that as settled.—Not that I wish to be arbitrary; but why should I waste your time in discussing what is inevitable?

UNDERSHAFT. You mean that you will stick at nothing not even the conversion of the Salvation Army to the worship of Dionysos.

CUSINS. The business of the Salvation Army is to save, not to wrangle about the name of the pathfinder. Dionysos or another: what does it matter?

UNDERSHAFT [rising and approaching him] Professor Cusins you are a young man after my own heart.

CUSINS. Mr Undershaft: you are, as far as I am able to gather, a most infernal old rascal; but you appeal very strongly to my sense of ironic humor.

Undershaft mutely offers his hand. They shake.

UNDERSHAFT [suddenly concentrating himself] And now to business.

CUSINS. Pardon me. We were discussing religion. Why go back to such an uninteresting and unimportant subject as business?

UNDERSHAFT. Religion is our business at present, because it is through religion alone that we can win Barbara.

CUSINS. Have you, too, fallen in love with Barbara?

UNDERSHAFT. Yes, with a father's love.

CUSINS. A father's love for a grown-up daughter is the most dangerous of all infatuations. I apologize for mentioning my own pale, coy, mistrustful fancy in the same breath with it.

UNDERSHAFT. Keep to the point. We have to win her; and we are neither of us Methodists.

CUSINS. That doesn't matter. The power Barbara wields here—the power that wields Barbara herself—is not Calvinism, not Presbyterianism, not Methodism—

UNDERSHAFT. Not Greek Paganism either, eh?

CUSINS. I admit that. Barbara is quite original in her religion.

UNDERSHAFT [triumphantly] Aha! Barbara Undershaft would be. Her inspiration comes from within herself.

CUSINS. How do you suppose it got there?

UNDERSHAFT [in towering excitement] It is the Undershaft inheritance. I shall hand on my torch to my daughter. She shall make my converts and preach my gospel.

CUSINS. What! Money and gunpowder!

UNDERSHAFT. Yes, money and gunpowder; freedom and power; command of life and command of death.

CUSINS [urbanely: trying to bring him down to earth] This is extremely interesting, Mr Undershaft. Of course you know that you are mad.

UNDERSHAFT [with redoubled force] And you?

CUSINS. Oh, mad as a hatter. You are welcome to my secret since I have discovered yours. But I am astonished. Can a madman make cannons?

UNDERSHAFT. Would anyone else than a madman make them? And now [with surging energy] question for question. Can a sane man translate Euripides?

CUSINS. No.

UNDERSHAFT [reining him by the shoulder] Can a sane woman make a man of a waster or a woman of a worm?

CUSINS [reeling before the storm] Father Colossus—Mammoth Millionaire—

UNDERSHAFT [pressing him] Are there two mad people or three in this Salvation shelter to-day?

CUSINS. You mean Barbara is as mad as we are!

UNDERSHAFT [pushing him lightly off and resuming his equanimity suddenly and completely] Pooh, Professor! let us call things by their proper names. I am a millionaire; you are a poet; Barbara is a savior of souls. What have we three to do with the common mob of slaves and idolaters? [He sits down again with a shrug of contempt for the mob].

CUSINS. Take care! Barbara is in love with the common people. So am I. Have you never felt the romance of that love?

UNDERSHAFT [cold and sardonic] Have you ever been in love with Poverty, like St Francis? Have you ever been in love with Dirt, like St Simeon? Have you ever been in love with disease and suffering, like our nurses and philanthropists? Such passions are not virtues, but the most unnatural of all the vices. This love of the common people may please an earl's granddaughter and a university professor; but I have been a common man and a poor man; and it has no romance for me. Leave it to the poor to pretend that poverty is a blessing: leave it to the coward to make a religion of his cowardice by preaching humility: we know better than that. We three must stand together above the common people: how else can we help their children to climb up beside us? Barbara must belong to us, not to the Salvation Army.

CUSINS. Well, I can only say that if you think you will get her away from the Salvation Army by talking to her as you have been talking to me, you don't know Barbara.

UNDERSHAFT. My friend: I never ask for what I can buy.

CUSINS [in a white fury] Do I understand you to imply that you can buy Barbara?

UNDERSHAFT. No; but I can buy the Salvation Army.

CUSINS. Quite impossible.

UNDERSHAFT. You shall see. All religious organizations exist by selling themselves to the rich.

CUSINS. Not the Army. That is the Church of the poor.

UNDERSHAFT. All the more reason for buying it.

CUSINS. I don't think you quite know what the Army does for the poor.

UNDERSHAFT. Oh yes I do. It draws their teeth: that is enough for me—as a man of business—

CUSINS. Nonsense! It makes them sober—

UNDERSHAFT. I prefer sober workmen. The profits are larger.

CUSINS. —honest—

UNDERSHAFT. Honest workmen are the most economical.

CUSINS. —attached to their homes—

UNDERSHAFT. So much the better: they will put up with anything sooner than change their shop.

CUSINS. —happy—

UNDERSHAFT. An invaluable safeguard against revolution.

CUSINS. —unselfish—

UNDERSHAFT. Indifferent to their own interests, which suits me exactly.

CUSINS. —with their thoughts on heavenly things—

UNDERSHAFT [rising] And not on Trade Unionism nor Socialism. Excellent.

CUSINS [revolted] You really are an infernal old rascal.

UNDERSHAFT [indicating Peter Shirley, who has just came from the shelter and strolled dejectedly down the yard between them] And this is an honest man!

SHIRLEY. Yes; and what av I got by it? [he passes on bitterly and sits on the form, in the corner of the penthouse].

Snobby Price, beaming sanctimoniously, and Jenny Hill, with a tambourine full of coppers, come from the shelter and go to the drum, on which Jenny begins to count the money.

UNDERSHAFT [replying to Shirley] Oh, your employers must have got a good deal by it from first to last. [He sits on the table, with one foot on the side form. Cusins, overwhelmed, sits down on the same form nearer the shelter. Barbara comes from the shelter to the middle of the yard. She is excited and a little overwrought].

BARBARA. We've just had a splendid experience meeting at the other gate in Cripps's lane. I've hardly ever seen them so much moved as they were by your confession, Mr Price.

PRICE. I could almost be glad of my past wickedness if I could believe that it would elp to keep hathers stright.

BARBARA. So it will, Snobby. How much, Jenny?

JENNY. Four and tenpence, Major.

BARBARA. Oh Snobby, if you had given your poor mother just one more kick, we should have got the whole five shillings!

PRICE. If she heard you say that, miss, she'd be sorry I didn't. But I'm glad. Oh what a joy it will be to her when she hears I'm saved!

UNDERSHAFT. Shall I contribute the odd twopence, Barbara? The millionaire's mite, eh? [He takes a couple of pennies from his pocket.]

BARBARA. How did you make that twopence?

UNDERSHAFT. As usual. By selling cannons, torpedoes, submarines, and my new patent Grand Duke hand grenade.

BARBARA. Put it back in your pocket. You can't buy your Salvation here for twopence: you must work it out.

UNDERSHAFT. Is twopence not enough? I can afford a little more, if you press me.

BARBARA. Two million millions would not be enough. There is bad blood on your hands; and nothing but good blood can cleanse them. Money is no use. Take it away. [She turns to Cusins]. Dolly: you must write another letter for me to the papers. [He makes a wry face]. Yes: I know you don't like it; but it must be done. The starvation this winter is beating us: everybody is unemployed. The General says we must close this shelter if we cant get more money. I force the collections at the meetings until I am ashamed, don't I, Snobby?

PRICE. It's a fair treat to see you work it, miss. The way you got them up from three-and-six to four-and-ten with that hymn, penny by penny and verse by verse, was a caution. Not a Cheap Jack on Mile End Waste could touch you at it.

BARBARA. Yes; but I wish we could do without it. I am getting at last to think more of the collection than of the people's souls. And what are those hatfuls of pence and halfpence? We want thousands! tens of thousands! hundreds of thousands! I want to convert people, not to be always begging for the Army in a way I'd die sooner than beg for myself.

UNDERSHAFT [in profound irony] Genuine unselfishness is capable of anything, my dear.

BARBARA [unsuspectingly, as she turns away to take the money from the drum and put it in a cash bag she carries] Yes, isn't it? [Undershaft looks sardonically at Cusins].

CUSINS [aside to Undershaft] Mephistopheles! Machiavelli!

BARBARA [tears coming into her eyes as she ties the bag and pockets it] How are we to feed them? I can't talk religion to a man with bodily hunger in his eyes. [Almost breaking down] It's frightful.

JENNY [running to her] Major, dear—

BARBARA [rebounding] No: don't comfort me. It will be all right. We shall get the money.

UNDERSHAFT. How?

JENNY. By praying for it, of course. Mrs Baines says she prayed for it last night; and she has never prayed for it in vain: never once. [She goes to the gate and looks out into the street].

BARBARA [who has dried her eyes and regained her composure] By the way, dad, Mrs Baines has come to march with us to our big meeting this afternoon; and she is very anxious to meet you, for some reason or other. Perhaps she'll convert you.

UNDERSHAFT. I shall be delighted, my dear.

JENNY [at the gate: excitedly] Major! Major! Here's that man back again.

BARBARA. What man?

JENNY. The man that hit me. Oh, I hope he's coming back to join us.

Bill Walker, with frost on his jacket, comes through the gate, his hands deep in his pockets and his chin sunk between his shoulders, like a cleaned-out gambler. He halts between Barbara and the drum.

BARBARA. Hullo, Bill! Back already!

BILL [nagging at her] Bin talkin ever sense, av you?

BARBARA. Pretty nearly. Well, has Todger paid you out for poor Jenny's jaw?

BILL. NO he ain't.

BARBARA. I thought your jacket looked a bit snowy.

BILL. So it is snowy. You want to know where the snow come from, don't you?

BARBARA. Yes.

BILL. Well, it come from off the ground in Parkinses Corner in Kennintahn. It got rubbed off be my shoulders: see?

BARBARA. Pity you didn't rub some off with your knees, Bill! That would have done you a lot of good.

BILL [with sour mirthless humor] I was saving another man's knees at the time. E was kneelin on my ed, so e was.

JENNY. Who was kneeling on your head?

BILL. Todger was. E was prayin for me: prayin comfortable with me as a carpet. So was Mog. So was the ole bloomin meetin. Mog she sez "O Lord break is stubborn spirit; but don't urt is dear art." That was wot she said. "Don't urt is dear art"! An er bloke—thirteen stun four!—kneelin wiv all is weight on me. Funny, ain't it?

JENNY. Oh no. We're so sorry, Mr Walker.

BARBARA [enjoying it frankly] Nonsense! of course it's funny. Served you right, Bill! You must have done something to him first.

BILL [doggedly] I did wot I said I'd do. I spit in is eye. E looks up at the sky and sez, "O that I should be fahnd worthy to be spit upon for the gospel's sake!" e sez; an Mog sez "Glory Allelloolier!"; an then e called me Brother, an dahned me as if I was a kid and e was me mother washin me a Setterda nawt. I adn't just no show wiv im at all. Arf the street prayed; an the tother arf larfed fit to split theirselves. [To Barbara] There! are you settisfawd nah?

BARBARA [her eyes dancing] Wish I'd been there, Bill.

BILL. Yes: you'd a got in a hextra bit o talk on me, wouldn't you?

JENNY. I'm so sorry, Mr. Walker.

BILL [fiercely] Don't you go bein sorry for me: you've no call. Listen ere. I broke your jawr.

JENNY. No, it didn't hurt me: indeed it didn't, except for a moment. It was only that I was frightened.

BILL. I don't want to be forgive be you, or be ennybody. Wot I did I'll pay for. I tried to get me own jawr broke to settisfaw you—

JENNY [distressed] Oh no—

BILL [impatiently] Tell y'I did: cawn't you listen to wot's bein told you? All I got be it was bein made a sight of in the public street for me pains. Well, if I cawn't settisfaw you one way, I can another. Listen ere! I ad two quid saved agen the frost; an I've a pahnd of it left. A mate o mine last week ad words with the Judy e's goin to marry. E give er wot-for; an e's bin fined fifteen bob. E ad a right to it er because they was goin to be marrid; but I adn't no right to it you; so put anather fawv bob on an call it a pahnd's worth. [He produces a sovereign]. Ere's the money. Take it; and let's av no more o your forgivin an prayin and your Major jawrin me. Let wot I done be done and paid for; and let there be a end of it.

JENNY. Oh, I couldn't take it, Mr. Walker. But if you would give a shilling or two to poor Rummy Mitchens! you really did hurt her; and she's old.

BILL [contemptuously] Not likely. I'd give her anather as soon as look at er. Let her av the lawr o me as she threatened! She ain't forgiven me: not mach. Wot I done to er is not on me mawnd—wot she [indicating Barbara] might call on me conscience—no more than stickin a pig. It's this Christian game o yours that I won't av played agen me: this bloomin forgivin an noggin an jawrin that makes a man that sore that iz lawf's a burdn to im. I won't av it, I tell you; so take your money and stop throwin your silly bashed face hup agen me.

JENNY. Major: may I take a little of it for the Army?

BARBARA. No: the Army is not to be bought. We want your soul, Bill; and we'll take nothing less.

BILL [bitterly] I know. It ain't enough. Me an me few shillins is not good enough for you. You're a earl's grendorter, you are. Nothin less than a underd pahnd for you.

UNDERSHAFT. Come, Barbara! you could do a great deal of good with a hundred pounds. If you will set this gentleman's mind at ease by taking his pound, I will give the other ninety-nine [Bill, astounded by such opulence, instinctively touches his cap].

BARBARA. Oh, you're too extravagant, papa. Bill offers twenty pieces of silver. All you need offer is the other ten. That will make the standard price to buy anybody who's for sale. I'm not; and the Army's not. [To Bill] You'll never have another quiet moment, Bill, until you come round to us. You can't stand out against your salvation.

BILL [sullenly] I cawn't stend aht agen music all wrastlers and artful tongued women. I've offered to pay. I can do no more. Take it or leave it. There it is. [He throws the sovereign on the drum, and sits down on the horse-trough. The coin fascinates Snobby Price, who takes an early opportunity of dropping his cap on it].

Mrs Baines comes from the shelter. She is dressed as a Salvation Army Commissioner. She is an earnest looking woman of about 40, with a caressing, urgent voice, and an appealing manner.

BARBARA. This is my father, Mrs Baines. [Undershaft comes from the table, taking his hat off with marked civility]. Try what you can do with him. He won't listen to me, because he remembers what a fool I was when I was a baby.

[She leaves them together and chats with Jenny].

MRS BAINES. Have you been shown over the shelter, Mr Undershaft? You know the work we're doing, of course.

UNDERSHAFT [very civilly] The whole nation knows it, Mrs Baines.

MRS BAINES. No, Sir: the whole nation does not know it, or we should not be crippled as we are for want of money to carry our work through the length and breadth of the land. Let me tell you that there would have been rioting this winter in London but for us.

UNDERSHAFT. You really think so?

MRS BAINES. I know it. I remember 1886, when you rich gentlemen hardened your hearts against the cry of the poor. They broke the windows of your clubs in Pall Mall.

UNDERSHAFT [gleaming with approval of their method] And the Mansion House Fund went up next day from thirty thousand pounds to seventy-nine thousand! I remember quite well.

MRS BAINES. Well, won't you help me to get at the people? They won't break windows then. Come here, Price. Let me show you to this gentleman [Price comes to be inspected]. Do you remember the window breaking?

PRICE. My ole father thought it was the revolution, ma'am.

MRS BAINES. Would you break windows now?

PRICE. Oh no ma'm. The windows of eaven av bin opened to me. I know now that the rich man is a sinner like myself.

RUMMY [appearing above at the loft door] Snobby Price!

SNOBBY. Wot is it?

RUMMY. Your mother's askin for you at the other gate in Crippses Lane. She's heard about your confession [Price turns pale].

MRS BAINES. Go, Mr. Price; and pray with her.

JENNY. You can go through the shelter, Snobby.

PRICE [to Mrs Baines] I couldn't face her now; ma'am, with all the weight of my sins fresh on me. Tell her she'll find her son at ome, waitin for her in prayer. [He skulks off through the gate, incidentally stealing the sovereign on his way out by picking up his cap from the drum].

MRS BAINES [with swimming eyes] You see how we take the anger and the bitterness against you out of their hearts, Mr Undershaft.

UNDERSHAFT. It is certainly most convenient and gratifying to all large employers of labor, Mrs Baines.

MRS BAINES. Barbara: Jenny: I have good news: most wonderful news. [Jenny runs to her]. My prayers have been answered. I told you they would, Jenny, didn't I?

JENNY. Yes, yes.

BARBARA [moving nearer to the drum] Have we got money enough to keep the shelter open?

MRS BAINES. I hope we shall have enough to keep all the shelters open. Lord Saxmundham has promised us five thousand pounds—

BARBARA. Hooray!

JENNY. Glory!

MRS BAINES. —if—

BARBARA. "If!" If what?

MRS BAINES. If five other gentlemen will give a thousand each to make it up to ten thousand.

BARBARA. Who is Lord Saxmundham? I never heard of him.

UNDERSHAFT [who has pricked up his ears at the peer's name, and is now watching Barbara curiously] A new creation, my dear. You have heard of Sir Horace Bodger?

BARBARA. Bodger! Do you mean the distiller? Bodger's whisky!

UNDERSHAFT. That is the man. He is one of the greatest of our public benefactors. He restored the cathedral at Hakington. They made him a baronet for that. He gave half a million to the funds of his party: they made him a baron for that.

SHIRLEY. What will they give him for the five thousand?

UNDERSHAFT. There is nothing left to give him. So the five thousand, I should think, is to save his soul.

MRS BAINES. Heaven grant it may! Oh Mr. Undershaft, you have some very rich friends. Can't you help us towards the other five thousand? We are going to hold a great meeting this afternoon at the Assembly

Hall in the Mile End Road. If I could only announce that one gentleman had come forward to support Lord Saxmundham, others would follow. Don't you know somebody? Couldn't you? Wouldn't you? [her eyes fill with tears] oh, think of those poor people, Mr Undershaft: think of how much it means to them, and how little to a great man like you.

UNDERSHAFT [sardonically gallant] Mrs Baines: you are irresistible. I can't disappoint you; and I can't deny myself the satisfaction of making Bodger pay up. You shall have your five thousand pounds.

MRS BAINES. Thank God!

UNDERSHAFT. You don't thank me?

MRS BAINES. Oh sir, don't try to be cynical: don't be ashamed of being a good man. The Lord will bless you abundantly; and our prayers will be like a strong fortification round you all the days of your life. [With a touch of caution] You will let me have the cheque to show at the meeting, won't you? Jenny: go in and fetch a pen and ink. [Jenny runs to the shelter door].

UNDERSHAFT. Do not disturb Miss Hill: I have a fountain pen. [Jenny halts. He sits at the table and writes the cheque. Cusins rises to make more room for him. They all watch him silently].

BILL [cynically, aside to Barbara, his voice and accent horribly debased] Wot prawce Selvytion nah?

BARBARA. Stop. [Undershaft stops writing: they all turn to her in surprise]. Mrs Baines: are you really going to take this money?

MRS BAINES [astonished] Why not, dear?

BARBARA. Why not! Do you know what my father is? Have you forgotten that Lord Saxmundham is Bodger the whisky man? Do you remember how we implored the County Council to stop him from writing Bodger's Whisky in letters of fire against the sky; so that the poor drinkruined creatures on the embankment could not wake up from their snatches of sleep without being reminded of their deadly thirst by that wicked sky sign? Do you know that the worst thing I have had to fight here is not the devil, but Bodger, Bodger,

Bodger, with his whisky, his distilleries, and his tied houses? Are you going to make our shelter another tied house for him, and ask me to keep it?

BILL. Rotten drunken whisky it is too.

MRS BAINES. Dear Barbara: Lord Saxmundham has a soul to be saved like any of us. If heaven has found the way to make a good use of his money, are we to set ourselves up against the answer to our prayers?

BARBARA. I know he has a soul to be saved. Let him come down here; and I'll do my best to help him to his salvation. But he wants to send his cheque down to buy us, and go on being as wicked as ever.

UNDERSHAFT [with a reasonableness which Cusins alone perceives to be ironical] My dear Barbara: alcohol is a very necessary article. It heals the sick—

BARBARA. It does nothing of the sort.

UNDERSHAFT. Well, it assists the doctor: that is perhaps a less questionable way of putting it. It makes life bearable to millions of people who could not endure their existence if they were quite sober. It enables Parliament to do things at eleven at night that no sane person would do at eleven in the morning. Is it Bodger's fault that this inestimable gift is deplorably abused by less than one per cent of the poor? [He turns again to the table; signs the cheque; and crosses it].

MRS BAINES. Barbara: will there be less drinking or more if all those poor souls we are saving come to-morrow and find the doors of our shelters shut in their faces? Lord Saxmundham gives us the money to stop drinking—to take his own business from him.

CUSINS [impishly] Pure self-sacrifice on Bodger's part, clearly! Bless dear Bodger! [Barbara almost breaks down as Adolpbus, too, fails her].

UNDERSHAFT [tearing out the cheque and pocketing the book as he rises and goes past Cusins to Mrs Baines] I also, Mrs Baines, may claim a little disinterestedness. Think of my business! think of the widows and orphans! the men and lads torn to pieces with shrapnel and poisoned with lyddite [Mrs Baines shrinks; but he goes on remorselessly]! the oceans of blood, not one drop of which is shed in a really just cause! the ravaged crops! the peaceful peasants forced, women and men, to till their fields under the fire of opposing armies on pain of starvation! the bad blood of the fierce little cowards at home who egg on others to fight for the gratification of their national vanity! All this makes money for me: I am never richer, never busier than when the papers are full of it. Well, it is your work to preach peace on earth and goodwill to men. [Mrs Baines's face lights up again]. Every convert you make is a vote against war. [Her lips move in prayer]. Yet I give you this money to help you to hasten my own commercial ruin. [He gives her the cheque].

CUSINS [mounting the form in an ecstasy of mischief] The millennium will be inaugurated by the unselfishness of Undershaft and Bodger. Oh be joyful! [He takes the drumsticks from his pockets and flourishes them].

MRS BAINES [taking the cheque] The longer I live the more proof I see that there is an Infinite Goodness that turns everything to the work of salvation sooner or later. Who would have thought that any good could have come out of war and drink? And yet their profits are brought today to the feet of salvation to do its blessed work. [She is affected to tears].

JENNY [running to Mrs Baines and throwing her arms round her] Oh dear! how blessed, how glorious it all is!

CUSINS [in a convulsion of irony] Let us seize this unspeakable moment. Let us march to the great meeting at once. Excuse me just an instant. [He rushes into the shelter. Jenny takes her tambourine from the drum head].

MRS BAINES. Mr Undershaft: have you ever seen a thousand people fall on their knees with one impulse and pray? Come with us to the meeting. Barbara shall tell them that the Army is saved, and saved through you.

CUSINS [returning impetuously from the shelter with a flag and a trombone, and coming between Mrs Baines and Undershaft] You shall carry the flag down the first street, Mrs Baines [he gives her the flag]. Mr Undershaft is a gifted trombonist: he shall intone an Olympian diapason to the West Ham Salvation March. [Aside to Undershaft, as he forces the trombone on him] Blow, Machiavelli, blow.

UNDERSHAFT [aside to him, as he takes the trombone] The trumpet in Zion! [Cusins rushes to the drum, which he takes up and puts on. Undershaft continues, aloud] I will do my best. I could vamp a bass if I knew the tune.

CUSINS. It is a wedding chorus from one of Donizetti's operas; but we have converted it. We convert everything to good here, including Bodger. You remember the chorus. "For thee immense rejoicing—immenso giubilo—immenso giubilo." [With drum obbligato] Rum tum ti tum tum, tum tum ti ta—

BARBARA. Dolly: you are breaking my heart.

CUSINS. What is a broken heart more or less here? Dionysos Undershaft has descended. I am possessed.

MRS BAINES. Come, Barbara: I must have my dear Major to carry the flag with me.

JENNY. Yes, yes, Major darling.

CUSINS [snatches the tambourine out of Jenny's hand and mutely offers it to Barbara].

BARBARA [coming forward a little as she puts the offer behind her with a shudder, whilst Cusins recklessly tosses the tambourine back to Jenny and goes to the gate] I can't come.

JENNY. Not come!

MRS BAINES [with tears in her eyes] Barbara: do you think I am wrong to take the money?

BARBARA [impulsively going to her and kissing her] No, no: God help you, dear, you must: you are saving the Army. Go; and may you have a great meeting!

JENNY. But arn't you coming?

BARBARA. No. [She begins taking off the silver brooch from her collar].

MRS BAINES. Barbara: what are you doing?

JENNY. Why are you taking your badge off? You can't be going to leave us, Major.

BARBARA [quietly] Father: come here.

UNDERSHAFT [coming to her] My dear! [Seeing that she is going to pin the badge on his collar, he retreats to the penthouse in some alarm].

BARBARA [following him] Don't be frightened. [She pins the badge on and steps back towards the table, showing him to the others] There! It's not much for 5000 pounds is it?

MRS BAINES. Barbara: if you won't come and pray with us, promise me you will pray for us.

BARBARA. I can't pray now. Perhaps I shall never pray again.

MRS BAINES. Barbara!

JENNY. Major!

BARBARA [almost delirious] I can't bear any more. Quick march!

CUSINS [calling to the procession in the street outside] Off we go. Play up, there! Immenso giubilo. [He gives the time with his drum; and the band strikes up the march, which rapidly becomes more distant as the procession moves briskly away].

MRS BAINES. I must go, dear. You're overworked: you will be all right tomorrow. We'll never lose you. Now Jenny: step out with the old flag. Blood and Fire! [She marches out through the gate with her flag].

JENNY. Glory Hallelujah! [flourishing her tambourine and marching].

UNDERSHAFT [to Cusins, as he marches out past him easing the slide of his trombone] "My ducats and my daughter"!

CUSINS [following him out] Money and gunpowder!

BARBARA. Drunkenness and Murder! My God: why hast thou forsaken me?

She sinks on the form with her face buried in her hands. The march passes away into silence. Bill Walker steals across to her.

BILL [taunting] Wot prawce Selvytion nah?

SHIRLEY. Don't you hit her when she's down.

BILL. She it me wen aw wiz dahn. Waw shouldn't I git a bit o me own back?

BARBARA [raising her head] I didn't take your money, Bill. [She crosses the yard to the gate and turns her back on the two men to hide her face from them].

BILL [sneering after her] Naow, it warn't enough for you. [Turning to the drum, he misses the money]. Ellow! If you ain't took it summun else az. Were's it gorn? Blame me if Jenny Ill didn't take it arter all!

RUMMY [screaming at him from the loft] You lie, you dirty blackguard! Snobby Price pinched it off the drum wen e took ap iz cap. I was ap ere all the time an see im do it.

BILL. Wot! Stowl maw money! Waw didn't you call thief on him, you silly old mucker you?

RUMMY. To serve you aht for ittin me acrost the face. It's cost y'pahnd, that az. [Raising a paean of squalid triumph] I done you. I'm even with you. I've ad it aht o y—. [Bill snatches up Shirley's mug and hurls it at her. She slams the loft door and vanishes. The mug smashes against the door and falls in fragments].

BILL [beginning to chuckle] Tell us, ole man, wot o'clock this morrun was it wen im as they call Snobby Prawce was sived?

BARBARA [turning to him more composedly, and with unspoiled sweetness] About half past twelve, Bill. And he pinched your pound at a quarter to two. I know. Well, you can't afford to lose it. I'll send it to you.

BILL [his voice and accent suddenly improving] Not if I was to starve for it. I ain't to be bought.

SHIRLEY. Ain't you? You'd sell yourself to the devil for a pint o beer; ony there ain't no devil to make the offer.

BILL [unshamed] So I would, mate, and often av, cheerful. But she cawn't buy me. [Approaching Barbara] You wanted my soul, did you? Well, you ain't got it.

BARBARA. I nearly got it, Bill. But we've sold it back to you for ten thousand pounds.

SHIRLEY. And dear at the money!

BARBARA. No, Peter: it was worth more than money.

BILL [salvationproof] It's no good: you cawn't get rahnd me nah. I don't blieve in it; and I've seen today that I was right. [Going] So long, old soupkitchener! Ta, ta, Major Earl's Grendorter! [Turning at the gate] Wot prawce Selvytion nah? Snobby Prawce! Ha! ha!

BARBARA [offering her hand] Goodbye, Bill.

BILL [taken aback, half plucks his cap off then shoves it on again defiantly] Git aht. [Barbara drops her hand, discouraged. He has a twinge of remorse]. But thet's aw rawt, you knaow. Nathink pasnl. Naow mellice. So long, Judy. [He goes].

BARBARA. No malice. So long, Bill.

SHIRLEY [shaking his head] You make too much of him, miss, in your innocence.

BARBARA [going to him] Peter: I'm like you now. Cleaned out, and lost my job.

SHIRLEY. You've youth an hope. That's two better than me. That's hope for you.

BARBARA. I'll get you a job, Peter, the youth will have to be enough for me. [She counts her money]. I have just enough left for two teas at Lockharts, a Rowton doss for you, and my tram and bus home. [He frowns and rises with offended pride. She takes his arm]. Don't be proud, Peter: it's sharing between friends. And promise me you'll talk to me and not let me cry. [She draws him towards the gate].

SHIRLEY. Well, I'm not accustomed to talk to the like of you—

BARBARA [urgently] Yes, yes: you must talk to me. Tell me about Tom Paine's books and Bradlaugh's lectures. Come along.

SHIRLEY. Ah, if you would only read Tom Paine in the proper spirit, miss! [They go out through the gate together].

ACT III

Next day after lunch Lady Britomart is writing in the library in Wilton Crescent. Sarah is reading in the armchair near the window. Barbara, in ordinary dresss, pale and brooding, is on the settee. Charley Lomax enters. Coming forward between the settee and the writing table, he starts on seeing Barbara fashionably attired and in low spirits.

LOMAX. You've left off your uniform!

Barbara says nothing; but an expression of pain passes over her face.

LADY BRITOMART [warning him in low tones to be careful] Charles!

LOMAX [much concerned, sitting down sympathetically on the settee beside Barbara] I'm awfully sorry, Barbara. You know I helped you all I could with the concertina and so forth. [Momentously] Still, I have never shut my eyes to the fact that there is a certain amount of tosh about the Salvation Army. Now the claims of the Church of England—

LADY BRITOMART. That's enough, Charles. Speak of something suited to your mental capacity.

LOMAX. But surely the Church of England is suited to all our capacities.

BARBARA [pressing his hand] Thank you for your sympathy, Cholly. Now go and spoon with Sarah.

LOMAX [rising and going to Sarah] How is my ownest today?

SARAH. I wish you wouldn't tell Cholly to do things, Barbara. He always comes straight and does them. Cholly: we're going to the works at Perivale St. Andrews this afternoon.

LOMAX. What works?

SARAH. The cannon works.

LOMAX. What! Your governor's shop!

SARAH. Yes.

LOMAX. Oh I say!

Cusins enters in poor condition. He also starts visibly when he sees Barbara without her uniform.

BARBARA. I expected you this morning, Dolly. Didn't you guess that?

CUSINS [sitting down beside her] I'm sorry. I have only just breakfasted.

SARAH. But we've just finished lunch.

BARBARA. Have you had one of your bad nights?

CUSINS. No: I had rather a good night: in fact, one of the most remarkable nights I have ever passed.

BARBARA. The meeting?

CUSINS. No: after the meeting.

LADY BRITOMART. You should have gone to bed after the meeting. What were you doing?

CUSINS. Drinking.

LADY BRITOMART. }{ Adolphus!
SARAH. }{ Dolly!
BARBARA. }{ Dolly!
LOMAX. }{ Oh I say!

LADY BRITOMART. What were you drinking, may I ask?

CUSINS. A most devilish kind of Spanish burgundy, warranted free from added alcohol: a Temperance burgundy in fact. Its richness in natural alcohol made any addition superfluous.

BARBARA. Are you joking, Dolly?

CUSINS [patiently] No. I have been making a night of it with the nominal head of this household: that is all.

LADY BRITOMART. Andrew made you drunk!

CUSINS. No: he only provided the wine. I think it was Dionysos who made me drunk. [To Barbara] I told you I was possessed.

LADY BRITOMART. You're not sober yet. Go home to bed at once.

CUSINS. I have never before ventured to reproach you, Lady Brit; but how could you marry the Prince of Darkness?

LADY BRITOMART. It was much more excusable to marry him than to get drunk with him. That is a new accomplishment of Andrew's, by the way. He usen't to drink.

CUSINS. He doesn't now. He only sat there and completed the wreck of my moral basis, the rout of my convictions, the purchase of my soul. He cares for you, Barbara. That is what makes him so dangerous to me.

BARBARA. That has nothing to do with it, Dolly. There are larger loves and diviner dreams than the fireside ones. You know that, don't you?

CUSINS. Yes: that is our understanding. I know it. I hold to it. Unless he can win me on that holier ground he may amuse me for a while; but he can get no deeper hold, strong as he is.

BARBARA. Keep to that; and the end will be right. Now tell me what happened at the meeting?

CUSINS. It was an amazing meeting. Mrs Baines almost died of emotion. Jenny Hill went stark mad with hysteria. The Prince of Darkness played his trombone like a madman: its brazen roarings were like the laughter of the damned. 117 conversions took place then and there. They prayed with the most touching sincerity and gratitude for Bodger, and for the anonymous donor of the 5000 pounds. Your father would not let his name be given.

LOMAX. That was rather fine of the old man, you know. Most chaps would have wanted the advertisement.

CUSINS. He said all the charitable institutions would be down on him like kites on a battle field if he gave his name.

LADY BRITOMART. That's Andrew all over. He never does a proper thing without giving an improper reason for it.

CUSINS. He convinced me that I have all my life been doing improper things for proper reasons.

LADY BRITOMART. Adolphus: now that Barbara has left the Salvation Army, you had better leave it too. I will not have you playing that drum in the streets.

CUSINS. Your orders are already obeyed, Lady Brit.

BARBARA. Dolly: were you ever really in earnest about it? Would you have joined if you had never seen me?

CUSINS [disingenuously] Well—er—well, possibly, as a collector of religions—

LOMAX [cunningly] Not as a drummer, though, you know. You are a very clearheaded brainy chap, Cholly; and it must have been apparent to you that there is a certain amount of tosh about—

LADY BRITOMART. Charles: if you must drivel, drivel like a grown-up man and not like a schoolboy.

LOMAX [out of countenance] Well, drivel is drivel, don't you know, whatever a man's age.

LADY BRITOMART. In good society in England, Charles, men drivel at all ages by repeating silly formulas with an air of wisdom. Schoolboys make their own formulas out of slang, like you. When they reach your age, and get political private secretaryships and things of that sort, they drop slang and get their formulas out of The Spectator or The Times. You had better confine yourself to The Times. You will find that there is a certain amount of tosh about The Times; but at least its language is reputable.

LOMAX [overwhelmed] You are so awfully strong-minded, Lady Brit—

LADY BRITOMART. Rubbish! [Morrison comes in]. What is it?

MORRISON. If you please, my lady, Mr Undershaft has just drove up to the door.

LADY BRITOMART. Well, let him in. [Morrison hesitates]. What's the matter with you?

MORRISON. Shall I announce him, my lady; or is he at home here, so to speak, my lady?

LADY BRITOMART. Announce him.

MORRISON. Thank you, my lady. You won't mind my asking, I hope. The occasion is in a manner of speaking new to me.

LADY BRITOMART. Quite right. Go and let him in.

MORRISON. Thank you, my lady. [He withdraws].

LADY BRITOMART. Children: go and get ready. [Sarah and Barbara go upstairs for their out-of-door wrap]. Charles: go and tell Stephen to come down here in five minutes: you will find him in the drawing room. [Charles goes]. Adolphus: tell them to send round the carriage in about fifteen minutes. [Adolphus goes].

MORRISON [at the door] Mr Undershaft.

Undershaft comes in. Morrison goes out.

UNDERSHAFT. Alone! How fortunate!

LADY BRITOMART [rising] Don't be sentimental, Andrew. Sit down. [She sits on the settee: he sits beside her, on her left. She comes to the point before he has time to breathe]. Sarah must have 800 pounds a year until Charles Lomax comes into his property. Barbara will need more, and need it permanently, because Adolphus hasn't any property.

UNDERSHAFT [resignedly] Yes, my dear: I will see to it. Anything else? for yourself, for instance?

LADY BRITOMART. I want to talk to you about Stephen.

UNDERSHAFT [rather wearily] Don't, my dear. Stephen doesn't interest me.

LADY BRITOMART. He does interest me. He is our son.

UNDERSHAFT. Do you really think so? He has induced us to bring him into the world; but he chose his parents very incongruously, I think. I see nothing of myself in him, and less of you.

LADY BRITOMART. Andrew: Stephen is an excellent son, and a most steady, capable, highminded young man. YOU are simply trying to find an excuse for disinheriting him.

UNDERSHAFT. My dear Biddy: the Undershaft tradition disinherits him. It would be dishonest of me to leave the cannon foundry to my son.

LADY BRITOMART. It would be most unnatural and improper of you to leave it to anyone else, Andrew. Do you suppose this wicked and immoral tradition can be kept up for ever? Do you pretend that Stephen could not carry on the foundry just as well as all the other sons of the big business houses?

UNDERSHAFT. Yes: he could learn the office routine without understanding the business, like all the other sons; and the firm would go on by its own momentum until the real Undershaft—probably an Italian or a German—would invent a new method and cut him out.

LADY BRITOMART. There is nothing that any Italian or German could do that Stephen could not do. And Stephen at least has breeding.

UNDERSHAFT. The son of a foundling! nonsense!

LADY BRITOMART. My son, Andrew! And even you may have good blood in your veins for all you know.

UNDERSHAFT. True. Probably I have. That is another argument in favor of a foundling.

LADY BRITOMART. Andrew: don't be aggravating. And don't be wicked. At present you are both.

UNDERSHAFT. This conversation is part of the Undershaft tradition, Biddy. Every Undershaft's wife has treated him to it ever since the house was founded. It is mere waste of breath. If the tradition be ever broken it will be for an abler man than Stephen.

LADY BRITOMART [pouting] Then go away.

UNDERSHAFT [deprecatory] Go away!

LADY BRITOMART. Yes: go away. If you will do nothing for Stephen, you are not wanted here. Go to your foundling, whoever he is; and look after him.

UNDERSHAFT. The fact is, Biddy—

LADY BRITOMART. Don't call me Biddy. I don't call you Andy.

UNDERSHAFT. I will not call my wife Britomart: it is not good sense. Seriously, my love, the Undershaft tradition has landed me in a difficulty. I am getting on in years; and my partner Lazarus has at last made a stand and insisted that the succession must be settled one way or the other; and of course he is quite right. You see, I haven't found a fit successor yet.

LADY BRITOMART [obstinately] There is Stephen.

UNDERSHAFT. That's just it: all the foundlings I can find are exactly like Stephen.

LADY BRITOMART. Andrew!!

UNDERSHAFT. I want a man with no relations and no schooling: that is, a man who would be out of the running altogether if he were not a strong man. And I can't find him. Every blessed foundling nowadays is snapped up in his infancy by Barnardo homes, or School Board officers, or Boards of Guardians; and if he shows the least ability, he is fastened on by schoolmasters; trained to win scholarships like a racehorse; crammed with secondhand ideas; drilled and disciplined in docility and what they call good taste; and lamed for life so that he is fit for nothing but teaching. If you want to keep the foundry in the family, you had better find an eligible foundling and marry him to Barbara.

LADY BRITOMART. Ah! Barbara! Your pet! You would sacrifice Stephen to Barbara.

UNDERSHAFT. Cheerfully. And you, my dear, would boil Barbara to make soup for Stephen.

LADY BRITOMART. Andrew: this is not a question of our likings and dislikings: it is a question of duty. It is your duty to make Stephen your successor.

UNDERSHAFT. Just as much as it is your duty to submit to your husband. Come, Biddy! these tricks of the governing class are of no use with me. I am one of the governing class myself; and it is waste of time giving tracts to a missionary. I have the power in this matter; and I am not to be humbugged into using it for your purposes.

LADY BRITOMART. Andrew: you can talk my head off; but you can't change wrong into right. And your tie is all on one side. Put it straight.

UNDERSHAFT [disconcerted] It won't stay unless it's pinned [he fumbles at it with childish grimaces]—

Stephen comes in.

STEPHEN [at the door] I beg your pardon [about to retire].

LADY BRITOMART. No: come in, Stephen. [Stephen comes forward to his mother's writing table.]

UNDERSHAFT [not very cordially] Good afternoon.

STEPHEN [coldly] Good afternoon.

UNDERSHAFT [to Lady Britomart] He knows all about the tradition, I suppose?

LADY BRITOMART. Yes. [To Stephen] It is what I told you last night, Stephen.

UNDERSHAFT [sulkily] I understand you want to come into the cannon business.

STEPHEN. I go into trade! Certainly not.

UNDERSHAFT [opening his eyes, greatly eased in mind and manner] Oh! in that case—!

LADY BRITOMART. Cannons are not trade, Stephen. They are enterprise.

STEPHEN. I have no intention of becoming a man of business in any sense. I have no capacity for business and no taste for it. I intend to devote myself to politics.

UNDERSHAFT [rising] My dear boy: this is an immense relief to me. And I trust it may prove an equally good thing for the country. I was afraid you would consider yourself disparaged and slighted. [He moves towards Stephen as if to shake hands with him].

LADY BRITOMART [rising and interposing] Stephen: I cannot allow you to throw away an enormous property like this.

STEPHEN [stiffly] Mother: there must be an end of treating me as a child, if you please. [Lady Britomart recoils, deeply wounded by his tone]. Until last night I did not take your attitude seriously, because I did not think you meant it seriously. But I find now that you left me in the dark as to matters which you should have explained to me years ago. I am extremely hurt and offended. Any further discussion of my intentions had better take place with my father, as between one man and another.

LADY BRITOMART. Stephen! [She sits down again; and her eyes fill with tears].

UNDERSHAFT [with grave compassion] You see, my dear, it is only the big men who can be treated as children.

STEPHEN. I am sorry, mother, that you have forced me—

UNDERSHAFT [stopping him] Yes, yes, yes, yes: that's all right, Stephen. She wont interfere with you any more: your independence is achieved: you have won your latchkey. Don't rub it in; and above all, don't apologize. [He resumes his seat]. Now what about your future, as between one man and another—I beg your pardon, Biddy: as between two men and a woman.

LADY BRITOMART [who has pulled herself together strongly] I quite understand, Stephen. By all means go your own way if you feel strong enough. [Stephen sits down magisterially in the chair at the writing table with an air of affirming his majority].

UNDERSHAFT. It is settled that you do not ask for the succession to the cannon business.

STEPHEN. I hope it is settled that I repudiate the cannon business.

UNDERSHAFT. Come, come! Don't be so devilishly sulky: it's boyish. Freedom should be generous. Besides, I owe you a fair start in life in exchange for disinheriting you. You can't become prime minister all at once. Haven't you a turn for something? What about literature, art and so forth?

STEPHEN. I have nothing of the artist about me, either in faculty or character, thank Heaven!

UNDERSHAFT. A philosopher, perhaps? Eh?

STEPHEN. I make no such ridiculous pretension.

UNDERSHAFT. Just so. Well, there is the army, the navy, the Church, the Bar. The Bar requires some ability. What about the Bar?

STEPHEN. I have not studied law. And I am afraid I have not the necessary push—I believe that is the name barristers give to their vulgarity—for success in pleading.

UNDERSHAFT. Rather a difficult case, Stephen. Hardly anything left but the stage, is there? [Stephen makes an impatient movement]. Well, come! is there anything you know or care for?

STEPHEN [rising and looking at him steadily] I know the difference between right and wrong.

UNDERSHAFT [hugely tickled] You don't say so! What! no capacity for business, no knowledge of law, no sympathy with art, no pretension to philosophy; only a simple knowledge of the secret that has puzzled all the philosophers, baffled all the lawyers, muddled all the men of business, and ruined most of the artists: the secret of right and wrong. Why, man, you're a genius, master of masters, a god! At twenty-four, too!

STEPHEN [keeping his temper with difficulty] You are pleased to be facetious. I pretend to nothing more than any honorable English gentleman claims as his birthright [he sits down angrily].

UNDERSHAFT. Oh, that's everybody's birthright. Look at poor little Jenny Hill, the Salvation lassie! she would think you were laughing at her if you asked her to stand up in the street and teach grammar or geography or mathematics or even drawingroom dancing; but it never occurs to her to doubt that she can teach morals and religion. You are all alike, you respectable people. You can't tell me the bursting strain of a ten-inch gun, which is a very simple matter; but you all think you can tell me the bursting strain of a man under temptation. You daren't handle high explosives; but you're all ready to handle honesty and truth and justice and the whole duty of man, and kill one another at that game. What a country! what a world!

LADY BRITOMART [uneasily] What do you think he had better do, Andrew?

UNDERSHAFT. Oh, just what he wants to do. He knows nothing; and he thinks he knows everything. That points clearly to a political career. Get him a private secretaryship to someone who can get him an Under Secretaryship; and then leave him alone. He will find his natural and proper place in the end on the Treasury bench.

STEPHEN [springing up again] I am sorry, sir, that you force me to forget the respect due to you as my father. I am an Englishman; and I will not hear the Government of my country insulted. [He thrusts his hands in his pockets, and walks angrily across to the window].

UNDERSHAFT [with a touch of brutality] The government of your country! I am the government of your country: I, and Lazarus. Do you suppose that you and half a dozen amateurs like you, sitting in a row in that foolish gabble shop, can govern Undershaft and Lazarus? No, my friend: you will do what pays US. You will make war when it suits us, and keep peace when it doesn't. You will find out that trade requires certain measures when we have decided on those measures. When I want anything to keep my dividends up, you will discover that my want is a national need. When other people want something to keep my dividends down, you will call out the police and military. And in return you shall have the support and applause of my newspapers, and the delight of imagining that you are a great statesman. Government of your country! Be off with you, my boy, and play with your caucuses and leading articles and historic parties and great leaders and burning questions and the rest of your toys. I am going back to my counting house to pay the piper and call the tune.

STEPHEN [actually smiling, and putting his hand on his father's shoulder with indulgent patronage] Really, my dear father, it is impossible to be angry with you. You don't know how absurd all this sounds to ME. You are very properly proud of having been industrious enough to make money; and it is greatly to your credit that you have made so much of it. But it has kept you in circles where you are valued for your money and deferred to for it, instead of in the doubtless very oldfashioned and behind-the-times public school and university where I formed my habits of mind. It is natural for you to think that money governs England; but you must allow me to think I know better.

UNDERSHAFT. And what does govern England, pray?

STEPHEN. Character, father, character.

UNDERSHAFT. Whose character? Yours or mine?

STEPHEN. Neither yours nor mine, father, but the best elements in the English national character.

UNDERSHAFT. Stephen: I've found your profession for you. You're a born journalist. I'll start you with a hightoned weekly review. There!

Stephen goes to the smaller writing table and busies himself with his letters.

Sarah, Barbara, Lomax, and Cusins come in ready for walking. Barbara crosses the room to the window and looks out. Cusins drifts amiably to the armchair, and Lomax remains near the door, whilst Sarah comes to her mother.

SARAH. Go and get ready, mamma: the carriage is waiting. [Lady Britomart leaves the room.]

UNDERSHAFT [to Sarah] Good day, my dear. Good afternoon, Mr. Lomax.

LOMAX [vaguely] Ahdedoo.

UNDERSHAFT [to Cusins] quite well after last night, Euripides, eh?

CUSINS. As well as can be expected.

UNDERSHAFT. That's right. [To Barbara] So you are coming to see my death and devastation factory, Barbara?

BARBARA [at the window] You came yesterday to see my salvation factory. I promised you a return visit.

LOMAX [coming forward between Sarah and Undershaft] You'll find it awfully interesting. I've been through the Woolwich Arsenal; and it gives you a ripping feeling of security, you know, to think of the lot of beggars we could kill if it came to fighting. [To Undershaft, with sudden solemnity] Still, it must be rather an awful reflection for you, from the religious point of view as it were. You're getting on, you know, and all that.

SARAH. You don't mind Cholly's imbecility, papa, do you?

LOMAX [much taken aback] Oh I say!

UNDERSHAFT. Mr Lomax looks at the matter in a very proper spirit, my dear.

LOMAX. Just so. That's all I meant, I assure you.

SARAH. Are you coming, Stephen?

STEPHEN. Well, I am rather busy—er— [Magnanimously] Oh well, yes: I'll come. That is, if there is room for me.

UNDERSHAFT. I can take two with me in a little motor I am experimenting with for field use. You won't mind its being rather unfashionable. It's not painted yet; but it's bullet proof.

LOMAX [appalled at the prospect of confronting Wilton Crescent in an unpainted motor] Oh I say!

SARAH. The carriage for me, thank you. Barbara doesn't mind what she's seen in.

LOMAX. I say, Dolly old chap: do you really mind the car being a guy? Because of course if you do I'll go in it. Still—

CUSINS. I prefer it.

LOMAX. Thanks awfully, old man. Come, Sarah. [He hurries out to secure his seat in the carriage. Sarah follows him].

CUSINS. [moodily walking across to Lady Britomart's writing table] Why are we two coming to this Works Department of Hell? that is what I ask myself.

BARBARA. I have always thought of it as a sort of pit where lost creatures with blackened faces stirred up smoky fires and were driven and tormented by my father. Is it like that, dad?

UNDERSHAFT [scandalized] My dear! It is a spotlessly clean and beautiful hillside town.

CUSINS. With a Methodist chapel? Oh do say theres a Methodist chapel.

UNDERSHAFT. There are two: a primitive one and a sophisticated one. There is even an Ethical Society; but it is not much patronized, as my men are all strongly religious. In the High Explosives Sheds they object to the presence of Agnostics as unsafe.

CUSINS. And yet they don't object to you!

BARBARA. Do they obey all your orders?

UNDERSHAFT. I never give them any orders. When I speak to one of them it is "Well, Jones, is the baby doing well? and has Mrs Jones made a good recovery?" "Nicely, thank you, sir." And that's all.

CUSINS. But Jones has to be kept in order. How do you maintain discipline among your men?

UNDERSHAFT. I don't. They do. You see, the one thing Jones won't stand is any rebellion from the man under him, or any assertion of social equality between the wife of the man with 4 shillings a week less than himself and Mrs Jones! Of course they all rebel against me, theoretically. Practically, every man of them keeps the man just below him in his place. I never meddle with them. I never bully them. I don't even bully Lazarus. I say that certain things are to be done; but I don't order anybody to do them. I don't say, mind you, that there is no ordering about and snubbing and even bullying. The men snub the boys and order them about; the carmen snub the sweepers; the artisans snub the unskilled laborers; the foremen drive and bully both the laborers and artisans; the assistant engineers find fault with the foremen; the chief engineers drop on the assistants; the departmental managers worry the chiefs; and the clerks have tall hats and hymnbooks and keep up the social tone by refusing to associate on equal terms with anybody. The result is a colossal profit, which comes to me.

CUSINS [revolted] You really are a—well, what I was saying yesterday.

BARBARA. What was he saying yesterday?

UNDERSHAFT. Never mind, my dear. He thinks I have made you unhappy. Have I?

BARBARA. Do you think I can be happy in this vulgar silly dress? I! who have worn the uniform. Do you understand what you have done to me? Yesterday I had a man's soul in my hand. I set him in the way of life with his face to salvation. But when we took your money he turned back to drunkenness and derision. [With intense conviction] I will never forgive you that. If I had a child, and you destroyed its body with your explosives—if you murdered Dolly with your horrible guns—I could forgive you if my forgiveness would open the gates of heaven to you. But to take a human soul from me, and turn it into the soul of a wolf! that is worse than any murder.

UNDERSHAFT. Does my daughter despair so easily? Can you strike a man to the heart and leave no mark on him?

BARBARA [her face lighting up] Oh, you are right: he can never be lost now: where was my faith?

CUSINS. Oh, clever clever devil!

BARBARA. You may be a devil; but God speaks through you sometimes. [She takes her father's hands and kisses them]. You have given me back my happiness: I feel it deep down now, though my spirit is troubled.

UNDERSHAFT. You have learnt something. That always feels at first as if you had lost something.

BARBARA. Well, take me to the factory of death, and let me learn something more. There must be some truth or other behind all this frightful irony. Come, Dolly. [She goes out].

CUSINS. My guardian angel! [To Undershaft] Avaunt! [He follows Barbara].

STEPHEN [quietly, at the writing table] You must not mind Cusins, father. He is a very amiable good fellow; but he is a Greek scholar and naturally a little eccentric.

UNDERSHAFT. Ah, quite so. Thank you, Stephen. Thank you. [He goes out].

Stephen smiles patronizingly; buttons his coat responsibly; and crosses the room to the door. Lady Britomart, dressed for out-of-doors, opens it before he reaches it. She looks round for the others; looks at Stephen; and turns to go without a word.

STEPHEN [embarrassed] Mother—

LADY BRITOMART. Don't be apologetic, Stephen. And don't forget that you have outgrown your mother. [She goes out].

Perivale St Andrews lies between two Middlesex hills, half climbing the northern one. It is an almost smokeless town of white walls, roofs of narrow green slates or red tiles, tall trees, domes, campaniles, and slender chimney shafts, beautifully situated and beautiful in itself. The best view of it is obtained from the crest of a slope about half a mile to the east, where the high explosives are dealt with. The foundry lies hidden in the depths between, the tops of its chimneys sprouting like huge skittles into the middle distance. Across the crest runs a platform of concrete, with a parapet which suggests a fortification, because there is a huge cannon of the obsolete Woolwich Infant pattern peering across it at the town. The cannon is mounted on an experimental gun carriage: possibly the original model of the Undershaft disappearing rampart gun alluded to by Stephen. The parapet has a high step inside which serves as a seat.

Barbara is leaning over the parapet, looking towards the town. On her right is the cannon; on her left the end of a shed raised on piles, with a ladder of three or four steps up to the door, which opens outwards and has a little wooden landing at the threshold, with a fire bucket in the corner of the landing. The parapet stops short of the shed, leaving a gap which is the beginning of the path down the hill through the foundry to the town. Behind the cannon is a trolley carrying a huge conical bombshell, with a red band painted on it. Further from the parapet, on the same side, is a deck chair, near the door of an office, which, like the sheds, is of the lightest possible construction.

Cusins arrives by the path from the town.

BARBARA. Well?

CUSINS. Not a ray of hope. Everything perfect, wonderful, real. It only needs a cathedral to be a heavenly city instead of a hellish one.

BARBARA. Have you found out whether they have done anything for old Peter Shirley.

CUSINS. They have found him a job as gatekeeper and timekeeper. He's frightfully miserable. He calls the timekeeping brainwork, and says he isn't used to it; and his gate lodge is so splendid that he's ashamed to use the rooms, and skulks in the scullery.

BARBARA. Poor Peter!

Stephen arrives from the town. He carries a fieldglass.

STEPHEN [enthusiastically] Have you two seen the place? Why did you leave us?

CUSINS. I wanted to see everything I was not intended to see; and Barbara wanted to make the men talk.

STEPHEN. Have you found anything discreditable?

CUSINS. No. They call him Dandy Andy and are proud of his being a cunning old rascal; but it's all horribly, frightfully, immorally, unanswerably perfect.

Sarah arrives.

SARAH. Heavens! what a place! [She crosses to the trolley]. Did you see the nursing home!? [She sits down on the shell].

STEPHEN. Did you see the libraries and schools!?

SARAH. Did you see the ballroom and the banqueting chamber in the Town Hall!?

STEPHEN. Have you gone into the insurance fund, the pension fund, the building society, the various applications of co-operation!?

Undershaft comes from the office, with a sheaf of telegrams in his hands.

UNDERSHAFT. Well, have you seen everything? I'm sorry I was called away. [Indicating the telegrams] News from Manchuria.

STEPHEN. Good news, I hope.

UNDERSHAFT. Very.

STEPHEN. Another Japanese victory?

UNDERSHAFT. Oh, I don't know. Which side wins does not concern us here. No: the good news is that the aerial battleship is a tremendous success. At the first trial it has wiped out a fort with three hundred soldiers in it.

CUSINS [from the platform] Dummy soldiers?

UNDERSHAFT. No: the real thing. [Cusins and Barbara exchange glances. Then Cusins sits on the step and buries his face in his hands. Barbara gravely lays her hand on his shoulder, and he looks up at her in a sort of whimsical desperation]. Well, Stephen, what do you think of the place?

STEPHEN. Oh, magnificent. A perfect triumph of organization. Frankly, my dear father, I have been a fool: I had no idea of what it all meant—of the wonderful forethought, the power of organization, the administrative capacity, the financial genius, the colossal capital it represents. I have been repeating to myself as I came through your streets "Peace hath her victories no less renowned than War." I have only one misgiving about it all.

UNDERSHAFT. Out with it.

STEPHEN. Well, I cannot help thinking that all this provision for every want of your workmen may sap their independence and weaken their sense of responsibility. And greatly as we enjoyed our tea at that splendid restaurant—how they gave us all that luxury and cake and jam and cream for threepence I really cannot imagine!—still you must remember that restaurants break up home life. Look at the continent, for instance! Are you sure so much pampering is really good for the men's characters?

UNDERSHAFT. Well you see, my dear boy, when you are organizing civilization you have to make up your mind whether trouble and anxiety are good things or not. If you decide that they are, then, I take it, you simply don't organize civilization; and there you are, with trouble and anxiety enough to make us all angels! But if you decide the other way, you may as well go through with it. However, Stephen, our characters are safe here. A sufficient dose of anxiety is always provided by the fact that we may be blown to smithereens at any moment.

SARAH. By the way, papa, where do you make the explosives?

UNDERSHAFT. In separate little sheds, like that one. When one of them blows up, it costs very little; and only the people quite close to it are killed.

Stephen, who is quite close to it, looks at it rather scaredly, and moves away quickly to the cannon. At the same moment the door of the shed is thrown abruptly open; and a foreman in overalls and list slippers comes out on the little landing and holds the door open for Lomax, who appears in the doorway.

LOMAX [with studied coolness] My good fellow: you needn't get into a state of nerves. Nothing's going to happen to you; and I suppose it wouldn't be the end of the world if anything did. A little bit of British pluck is what you want, old chap. [He descends and strolls across to Sarah].

UNDERSHAFT [to the foreman] Anything wrong, Bilton?

BILTON [with ironic calm] Gentleman walked into the high explosives shed and lit a cigaret, sir: that's all.

UNDERSHAFT. Ah, quite so. [To Lomax] Do you happen to remember what you did with the match?

LOMAX. Oh come! I'm not a fool. I took jolly good care to blow it out before I chucked it away.

BILTON. The top of it was red hot inside, sir.

LOMAX. Well, suppose it was! I didn't chuck it into any of your messes.

UNDERSHAFT. Think no more of it, Mr Lomax. By the way, would you mind lending me your matches?

LOMAX [offering his box] Certainly.

UNDERSHAFT. Thanks. [He pockets the matches].

LOMAX [lecturing to the company generally] You know, these high explosives don't go off like gunpowder, except when they're in a gun. When they're spread loose, you can put a match to them without the least risk: they just burn quietly like a bit of paper. [Warming to the scientific interest of the subject] Did you know that Undershaft? Have you ever tried?

UNDERSHAFT. Not on a large scale, Mr Lomax. Bilton will give you a sample of gun cotton when you are leaving if you ask him. You can experiment with it at home. [Bilton looks puzzled].

SARAH. Bilton will do nothing of the sort, papa. I suppose it's your business to blow up the Russians and Japs; but you might really stop short of blowing up poor Cholly. [Bilton gives it up and retires into the shed].

LOMAX. My ownest, there is no danger. [He sits beside her on the shell].

Lady Britomart arrives from the town with a bouquet.

LADY BRITOMART [coming impetuously between Undershaft and the deck chair] Andrew: you shouldn't have let me see this place.

UNDERSHAFT. Why, my dear?

LADY BRITOMART. Never mind why: you shouldn't have: that's all. To think of all that [indicating the town] being yours! and that you have kept it to yourself all these years!

UNDERSHAFT. It does not belong to me. I belong to it. It is the Undershaft inheritance.

LADY BRITOMART. It is not. Your ridiculous cannons and that noisy banging foundry may be the Undershaft inheritance; but all that plate and linen, all that furniture and those houses and orchards and gardens belong to us. They belong to me: they are not a man's business. I won't give them up. You must be out of your senses to throw them all away; and if you persist in such folly, I will call in a doctor.

UNDERSHAFT [stooping to smell the bouquet] Where did you get the flowers, my dear?

LADY BRITOMART. Your men presented them to me in your William Morris Labor Church.

CUSINS [springing up] Oh! It needed only that. A Labor Church!

LADY BRITOMART. Yes, with Morris's words in mosaic letters ten feet high round the dome. NO MAN IS GOOD ENOUGH TO BE ANOTH-

ER MAN'S MASTER. The cynicism of it!

UNDERSHAFT. It shocked the men at first, I am afraid. But now they take no more notice of it than of the ten commandments in church.

LADY BRITOMART. Andrew: you are trying to put me off the subject of the inheritance by profane jokes. Well, you shan't. I don't ask it any longer for Stephen: he has inherited far too much of your perversity to be fit for it. But Barbara has rights as well as Stephen. Why should not Adolphus succeed to the inheritance? I could manage the town for him; and he can look after the cannons, if they are really necessary.

UNDERSHAFT. I should ask nothing better if Adolphus were a foundling. He is exactly the sort of new blood that is wanted in English business. But he's not a foundling; and there's an end of it.

CUSINS [diplomatically] Not quite. [They all turn and stare at him. He comes from the platform past the shed to Undershaft]. I think—Mind! I am not committing myself in any way as to my future course—but I think the foundling difficulty can be got over.

UNDERSHAFT. What do you mean?

CUSINS. Well, I have something to say which is in the nature of a confession.

SARAH. }
LADY BRITOMART. } Confession!
BARBARA. }
STEPHEN. }
LOMAX. Oh I say!

CUSINS. Yes, a confession. Listen, all. Until I met Barbara I thought myself in the main an honorable, truthful man, because I wanted the approval of my conscience more than I wanted anything else. But the moment I saw Barbara, I wanted her far more than the approval of my conscience.

LADY BRITOMART. Adolphus!

CUSINS. It is true. You accused me yourself, Lady Brit, of joining the Army to worship Barbara; and so I did. She bought my soul like a flower at a street corner; but she bought it for herself.

UNDERSHAFT. What! Not for Dionysos or another?

CUSINS. Dionysos and all the others are in herself. I adored what was divine in her, and was therefore a true worshipper. But I was romantic about her too. I thought she was a woman of the people, and that a marriage with a professor of Greek would be far beyond the wildest social ambitions of her rank.

LADY BRITOMART. Adolphus!!

LOMAX. Oh I say!!!

CUSINS. When I learnt the horrible truth—

LADY BRITOMART. What do you mean by the horrible truth, pray?

CUSINS. That she was enormously rich; that her grandfather was an earl; that her father was the Prince of Darkness—

UNDERSHAFT. Chut!

CUSINS.—and that I was only an adventurer trying to catch a rich wife, then I stooped to deceive about my birth.

LADY BRITOMART. Your birth! Now Adolphus, don't dare to make up a wicked story for the sake of these wretched cannons. Remember: I have seen photographs of your parents; and the Agent General for South Western Australia knows them personally and has assured me that they are most respectable married people.

CUSINS. So they are in Australia; but here they are outcasts. Their marriage is legal in Australia, but not in England. My mother is my father's deceased wife's sister; and in this island I am consequently a foundling. [Sensation]. Is the subterfuge good enough, Machiavelli?

UNDERSHAFT [thoughtfully] Biddy: this may be a way out of the difficulty.

LADY BRITOMART. Stuff! A man can't make cannons any the better for being his own cousin instead of his proper self [she sits down in the deck chair with a bounce that expresses her downright contempt for their casuistry.]

UNDERSHAFT [to Cusins] You are an educated man. That is against the tradition.

CUSINS. Once in ten thousand times it happens that the schoolboy is a born master of what they try to teach him. Greek has not destroyed my mind: it has nourished it. Besides, I did not learn it at an English public school.

UNDERSHAFT. Hm! Well, I cannot afford to be too particular: you have cornered the foundling market. Let it pass. You are eligible, Euripides: you are eligible.

BARBARA [coming from the platform and interposing between Cusins and Undershaft] Dolly: yesterday morning, when Stephen told us all about the tradition, you became very silent; and you have been strange and excited ever since. Were you thinking of your birth then?

CUSINS. When the finger of Destiny suddenly points at a man in the middle of his breakfast, it makes him thoughtful. [Barbara turns away sadly and stands near her mother, listening perturbedly].

UNDERSHAFT. Aha! You have had your eye on the business, my young friend, have you?

CUSINS. Take care! There is an abyss of moral horror between me and your accursed aerial battleships.

UNDERSHAFT. Never mind the abyss for the present. Let us settle the practical details and leave your final decision open. You know that you will have to change your name. Do you object to that?

CUSINS. Would any man named Adolphus—any man called Dolly!—object to be called something else?

UNDERSHAFT. Good. Now, as to money! I propose to treat you handsomely from the beginning. You shall start at a thousand a year.

CUSINS. [with sudden heat, his spectacles twinkling with mischief] A thousand! You dare offer a miserable thousand to the son-in-law of a millionaire! No, by Heavens, Machiavelli! you shall not cheat me. You cannot do without me; and I can do without you. I must have two thousand five hundred a year for two years. At the end of that time, if I am a failure, I go. But if I am a success, and stay on, you must give me the other five thousand.

UNDERSHAFT. What other five thousand?

CUSINS. To make the two years up to five thousand a year. The two thousand five hundred is only half pay in case I should turn out a failure. The third year I must have ten per cent on the profits.

UNDERSHAFT [taken aback] Ten per cent! Why, man, do you know what my profits are?

CUSINS. Enormous, I hope: otherwise I shall require twenty-five per cent.

UNDERSHAFT. But, Mr Cusins, this is a serious matter of business. You are not bringing any capital into the concern.

CUSINS. What! no capital! Is my mastery of Greek no capital? Is my access to the subtlest thought, the loftiest poetry yet attained by humanity, no capital? my character! my intellect! my life! my career! what Barbara calls my soul! are these no capital? Say another word; and I double my salary.

UNDERSHAFT. Be reasonable—

CUSINS [peremptorily] Mr Undershaft: you have my terms. Take them or leave them.

UNDERSHAFT [recovering himself] Very well. I note your terms; and I offer you half.

CUSINS [disgusted] Half!

UNDERSHAFT [firmly] Half.

CUSINS. You call yourself a gentleman; and you offer me half!!

UNDERSHAFT. I do not call myself a gentleman; but I offer you half.

CUSINS. This to your future partner! your successor! your son-in-law!

BARBARA. You are selling your own soul, Dolly, not mine. Leave me out of the bargain, please.

UNDERSHAFT. Come! I will go a step further for Barbara's sake. I will give you three fifths; but that is my last word.

CUSINS. Done!

LOMAX. Done in the eye. Why, I only get eight hundred, you know.

CUSINS. By the way, Mac, I am a classical scholar, not an arithmetical one. Is three fifths more than half or less?

UNDERSHAFT. More, of course.

CUSINS. I would have taken two hundred and fifty. How you can succeed in business when you are willing to pay all that money to a University don who is obviously not worth a junior clerk's wages!—well! What will Lazarus say?

UNDERSHAFT. Lazarus is a gentle romantic Jew who cares for nothing but string quartets and stalls at fashionable theatres. He will get the credit of your rapacity in money matters, as he has hitherto had the credit of mine. You are a shark of the first order, Euripides. So much the better for the firm!

BARBARA. Is the bargain closed, Dolly? Does your soul belong to him now?

CUSINS. No: the price is settled: that is all. The real tug of war is still to come. What about the moral question?

LADY BRITOMART. There is no moral question in the matter at all, Adolphus. You must simply sell cannons and weapons to people whose cause is right and just, and refuse them to foreigners and criminals.

UNDERSHAFT [determinedly] No: none of that. You must keep the true faith of an Armorer, or you don't come in here.

CUSINS. What on earth is the true faith of an Armorer?

UNDERSHAFT. To give arms to all men who offer an honest price for them, without respect of persons or principles: to aristocrat and republican, to Nihilist and Tsar, to Capitalist and Socialist, to Protestant and Catholic, to burglar and policeman, to black man, white man and yellow man, to all sorts and conditions, all nationalities, all faiths, all follies, all causes and all crimes. The first Undershaft wrote up in his shop IF GOD GAVE THE HAND, LET NOT MAN WITHHOLD THE SWORD. The second wrote up ALL HAVE THE RIGHT TO FIGHT: NONE HAVE THE RIGHT TO JUDGE. The third wrote up TO MAN THE WEAPON: TO HEAVEN THE VICTORY. The fourth had no literary turn; so he did not write up anything; but he sold cannons to Napoleon under the nose of George the Third. The fifth wrote up PEACE SHALL NOT PREVAIL SAVE WITH A SWORD IN HER HAND. The sixth, my master, was the best of all. He wrote up NOTHING IS EVER DONE IN THIS WORLD UNTIL MEN ARE PREPARED TO KILL ONE ANOTHER IF IT IS NOT DONE. After that, there was nothing left for the seventh to say. So he wrote up, simply, UNASHAMED.

CUSINS. My good Machiavelli, I shall certainly write something up on the wall; only, as I shall write it in Greek, you won't be able to read it. But as to your Armorer's faith, if I take my neck out of the noose of my own morality I am not going to put it into the noose of yours. I shall sell cannons to whom I please and refuse them to whom I please. So there!

UNDERSHAFT. From the moment when you become Andrew Undershaft, you will never do as you please again. Don't come here lusting for power, young man.

CUSINS. If power were my aim I should not come here for it. YOU have no power.

UNDERSHAFT. None of my own, certainly.

CUSINS. I have more power than you, more will. You do not drive this place: it drives you. And what drives the place?

UNDERSHAFT [enigmatically] A will of which I am a part.

BARBARA [startled] Father! Do you know what you are saying; or are you laying a snare for my soul?

CUSINS. Don't listen to his metaphysics, Barbara. The place is driven by the most rascally part of society, the money hunters, the pleasure hunters, the military promotion hunters; and he is their slave.

UNDERSHAFT. Not necessarily. Remember the Armorer's Faith. I will take an order from a good man as cheerfully as from a bad one. If you good people prefer preaching and shirking to buying my weapons and fighting the rascals, don't blame me. I can make cannons: I cannot make courage and conviction. Bah! You tire me, Euripides, with your morality mongering. Ask Barbara: SHE understands. [He suddenly takes Barbara's hands, and looks powerfully into her eyes]. Tell him, my love, what power really means.

BARBARA [hypnotized] Before I joined the Salvation Army, I was in my own power; and the consequence was that I never knew what to do with myself. When I joined it, I had not time enough for all the things I had to do.

UNDERSHAFT [approvingly] Just so. And why was that, do you suppose?

BARBARA. Yesterday I should have said, because I was in the power of God. [She resumes her self-possession, withdrawing her hands from his with a power equal to his own]. But you came and showed me that I was in the power of Bodger and Undershaft. Today I feel—oh! how can I put it into words? Sarah: do you remember the earthquake at Cannes, when we were little children?—how little the surprise of the first shock mattered compared to the dread and horror of waiting for the second? That is how I feel in this place today. I stood on the rock I thought eternal; and without a word of warning it reeled and crumbled under me. I was safe with an infinite wisdom watching me, an army marching to Salvation with me; and in a moment, at a stroke of your pen in a cheque book, I stood alone; and the heavens were empty. That was the first shock of the earthquake: I am waiting for the second.

UNDERSHAFT. Come, come, my daughter! Don't make too much of your little tinpot tragedy. What do we do here when we spend years of work and thought and thousands of pounds of solid cash on a new gun or an aerial battleship that turns out just a hairsbreadth wrong after all? Scrap it. Scrap it without wasting another hour or another pound on it. Well, you have made for yourself something that you call a morality or a religion or what not. It doesn't fit the facts. Well, scrap it. Scrap it and get one that does fit. That is what is wrong with the world at present. It scraps its obsolete steam engines and dynamos; but it won't scrap its old prejudices and its old moralities and its old religions and its old political constitutions. What's the result? In machinery it does very well; but in morals and religion and politics it is working at a loss that brings it nearer bankruptcy every year. Don't persist in that folly. If your old religion broke down yesterday, get a newer and a better one for tomorrow.

BARBARA. Oh how gladly I would take a better one to my soul! But you offer me a worse one. [Turning on him with sudden vehemence]. Justify yourself: show me some light through the darkness of this dreadful place, with its beautifully clean workshops, and respectable workmen, and model homes.

UNDERSHAFT. Cleanliness and respectability do not need justification, Barbara: they justify themselves. I see no darkness here, no dreadfulness. In your Salvation shelter I saw poverty, misery, cold and hunger. You gave them bread and treacle and dreams of heaven. I give from thirty shillings a week to twelve thousand a year. They find their own dreams; but I look after the drainage.

BARBARA. And their souls?

UNDERSHAFT. I save their souls just as I saved yours.

BARBARA [revolted] You saved my soul! What do you mean?

UNDERSHAFT. I fed you and clothed you and housed you. I took care that you should have money enough to live handsomely—more than enough; so that you could be wasteful, careless, generous. That saved your soul from the seven deadly sins.

BARBARA [bewildered] The seven deadly sins!

UNDERSHAFT. Yes, the deadly seven. [Counting on his fingers] Food, clothing, firing, rent, taxes, respectability and children. Nothing can lift those seven millstones from Man's neck but money; and the spirit cannot soar until the millstones are lifted. I lifted them from your spirit. I enabled Barbara to become Major Barbara; and I saved her from the crime of poverty.

CUSINS. Do you call poverty a crime?

UNDERSHAFT. The worst of crimes. All the other crimes are virtues beside it: all the other dishonors are chivalry itself by comparison. Poverty blights whole cities; spreads horrible pestilences; strikes dead the very souls of all who come within sight, sound or smell of it. What you call crime is nothing: a murder here and a theft there, a blow now and a curse then: what do they matter? they are only the accidents and illnesses of life: there are not fifty genuine professional criminals in London. But there are millions of poor people, abject people, dirty people, ill fed, ill clothed people. They poison us morally and physically: they kill the happiness of society: they force us to do away with our own liberties and to organize unnatural cruelties for fear they should rise against us and drag us down into their abyss. Only fools fear crime: we all fear poverty. Pah! [turning on Barbara] you talk of your half-saved ruffian in West Ham: you accuse me of dragging his soul back to perdition. Well, bring him to me here; and I will drag his soul back again to salvation for you. Not by words and dreams; but by thirty-eight shillings a week, a sound house in a handsome street, and a permanent job. In three weeks he will have a fancy waistcoat; in three months a tall hat and a chapel sitting; before the end of the year he will shake hands with a duchess at a Primrose League meeting, and join the Conservative Party.

BARBARA. And will he be the better for that?

UNDERSHAFT. You know he will. Don't be a hypocrite, Barbara. He will be better fed, better housed, better clothed, better behaved; and his children will be pounds heavier and bigger. That will be better than an American cloth mattress in a shelter, chopping firewood, eating bread and treacle, and being forced to kneel down from time to time to thank heaven for it: knee drill, I think you call it. It is cheap work converting starving men with a Bible in one hand and a slice of bread in the other. I will undertake to convert West Ham to Mahometanism on the same terms. Try your hand on my men: their souls are hungry because their bodies are full.

BARBARA. And leave the east end to starve?

UNDERSHAFT [his energetic tone dropping into one of bitter and brooding remembrance] I was an east ender. I moralized and starved until one day I swore that I would be a fullfed free man at all costs—that nothing should stop me except a bullet, neither reason nor morals nor the lives of other men. I said "Thou shalt starve ere I starve"; and with that word I became free and great. I was a dangerous man until I had my will: now I am a useful, beneficent, kindly person. That is the history of most self-made millionaires, I fancy. When it is the history of every Englishman we shall have an England worth living in.

LADY BRITOMART. Stop making speeches, Andrew. This is not the place for them.

UNDERSHAFT [punctured] My dear: I have no other means of conveying my ideas.

LADY BRITOMART. Your ideas are nonsense. You got oil because you were selfish and unscrupulous.

UNDERSHAFT. Not at all. I had the strongest scruples about poverty and starvation. Your moralists are quite unscrupulous about both: they make virtues of them. I had rather be a thief than a pauper. I had rather be a murderer than a slave. I don't want to be either; but if you force the alternative on me, then, by Heaven, I'll choose the braver and more moral one. I hate poverty and slavery worse than any other crimes whatsoever. And let me tell you this. Poverty and slavery have stood up for centuries to your sermons and leading articles: they will not stand up to my machine guns. Don't preach at them: don't reason with them. Kill them.

BARBARA. Killing. Is that your remedy for everything?

UNDERSHAFT. It is the final test of conviction, the only lever strong enough to overturn a social system, the only way of saying Must. Let six hundred and seventy fools loose in the street; and three policemen can scatter them. But huddle them together in a certain house in Westminster; and let them go through certain ceremonies and call themselves certain names until at last they get the courage to kill; and your six hundred and seventy fools become a government. Your pious mob fills up ballot papers and imagines it is governing its masters; but the ballot paper that really governs is the paper that has a bullet wrapped up in it.

CUSINS. That is perhaps why, like most intelligent people, I never vote.

UNDERSHAFT Vote! Bah! When you vote, you only change the names of the cabinet. When you shoot, you pull down governments, inaugurate new epochs, abolish old orders and set up new. Is that historically true, Mr Learned Man, or is it not?

CUSINS. It is historically true. I loathe having to admit it. I repudiate your sentiments. I abhor your nature. I defy you in every possible way. Still, it is true. But it ought not to be true.

UNDERSHAFT. Ought, ought, ought, ought, ought! Are you going to spend your life saying ought, like the rest of our moralists? Turn your oughts into shalls, man. Come and make explosives with me. Whatever can blow men up can blow society up. The history of the world is the history of those who had courage enough to embrace this truth. Have you the courage to embrace it, Barbara?

LADY BRITOMART. Barbara, I positively forbid you to listen to your father's abominable wickedness. And you, Adolphus, ought to know better than to go about saying that wrong things are true. What does it matter whether they are true if they are wrong?

UNDERSHAFT. What does it matter whether they are wrong if they are true?

LADY BRITOMART [rising] Children: come home instantly. Andrew: I am exceedingly sorry I allowed you to call on us. You are wickeder than ever. Come at once.

BARBARA [shaking her head] It's no use running away from wicked people, mamma.

LADY BRITOMART. It is every use. It shows your disapprobation of them.

BARBARA. It does not save them.

LADY BRITOMART. I can see that you are going to disobey me. Sarah: are you coming home or are you not?

SARAH. I daresay it's very wicked of papa to make cannons; but I don't think I shall cut him on that account.

LOMAX [pouring oil on the troubled waters] The fact is, you know, there is a certain amount of tosh about this notion of wickedness. It doesn't work. You must look at facts. Not that I would say a word in favor of anything wrong; but then, you see, all sorts of chaps are always doing all sorts of things; and we have to fit them in somehow, don't you know. What I mean is that you can't go cutting everybody; and that's about what it comes to. [Their rapt attention to his eloquence makes him nervous] Perhaps I don't make myself clear.

LADY BRITOMART. You are lucidity itself, Charles. Because Andrew is successful and has plenty of money to give to Sarah, you will flatter him and encourage him in his wickedness.

LOMAX [unruffled] Well, where the carcase is, there will the eagles be gathered, don't you know. [To Undershaft] Eh? What?

UNDERSHAFT. Precisely. By the way, may I call you Charles?

LOMAX. Delighted. Cholly is the usual ticket.

UNDERSHAFT [to Lady Britomart] Biddy—

LADY BRITOMART [violently] Don't dare call me Biddy. Charles Lomax: you are a fool. Adolphus Cusins: you are a Jesuit. Stephen: you are a prig. Barbara: you are a lunatic. Andrew: you are a vulgar tradesman. Now you all know my opinion; and my conscience is clear, at all events [she sits down again with a vehemence that almost wrecks the chair].

UNDERSHAFT. My dear, you are the incarnation of morality. [She snorts]. Your conscience is clear and your duty done when you have called everybody names. Come, Euripides! it is getting late; and we all want to get home. Make up your mind.

CUSINS. Understand this, you old demon—

LADY BRITOMART. Adolphus!

UNDERSHAFT. Let him alone, Biddy. Proceed, Euripides.

CUSINS. You have me in a horrible dilemma. I want Barbara.

UNDERSHAFT. Like all young men, you greatly exaggerate the difference between one young woman and another.

BARBARA. Quite true, Dolly.

CUSINS. I also want to avoid being a rascal.

UNDERSHAFT [with biting contempt] You lust for personal righteousness, for self-approval, for what you call a good conscience, for what Barbara calls salvation, for what I call patronizing people who are not so lucky as yourself.

CUSINS. I do not: all the poet in me recoils from being a good man. But there are things in me that I must reckon with: pity—

UNDERSHAFT. Pity! The scavenger of misery.

CUSINS. Well, love.

UNDERSHAFT. I know. You love the needy and the outcast: you love the oppressed races, the negro, the Indian ryot, the Pole, the Irishman. Do you love the Japanese? Do you love the Germans? Do you love the English?

CUSINS. No. Every true Englishman detests the English. We are the wickedest nation on earth; and our success is a moral horror.

UNDERSHAFT. That is what comes of your gospel of love, is it?

CUSINS. May I not love even my father-in-law?

UNDERSHAFT. Who wants your love, man? By what right do you take the liberty of offering it to me? I will have your due heed and respect, or I will kill you. But your love! Damn your impertinence!

CUSINS [grinning] I may not be able to control my affections, Mac.

UNDERSHAFT. You are fencing, Euripides. You are weakening: your grip is slipping. Come! try your last weapon. Pity and love have broken in your hand: forgiveness is still left.

CUSINS. No: forgiveness is a beggar's refuge. I am with you there: we must pay our debts.

UNDERSHAFT. Well said. Come! you will suit me. Remember the words of Plato.

CUSINS [starting] Plato! You dare quote Plato to me!

UNDERSHAFT. Plato says, my friend, that society cannot be saved until either the Professors of Greek take to making gunpowder, or else the makers of gunpowder become Professors of Greek.

CUSINS. Oh, tempter, cunning tempter!

UNDERSHAFT. Come! choose, man, choose.

CUSINS. But perhaps Barbara will not marry me if I make the wrong choice.

BARBARA. Perhaps not.

CUSINS [desperately perplexed] You hear—

BARBARA. Father: do you love nobody?

UNDERSHAFT. I love my best friend.

LADY BRITOMART. And who is that, pray?

UNDERSHAFT. My bravest enemy. That is the man who keeps me up to the mark.

CUSINS. You know, the creature is really a sort of poet in his way. Suppose he is a great man, after all!

UNDERSHAFT. Suppose you stop talking and make up your mind, my young friend.

CUSINS. But you are driving me against my nature. I hate war.

UNDERSHAFT. Hatred is the coward's revenge for being intimidated. Dare you make war on war? Here are the means: my friend Mr Lomax is sitting on them.

LOMAX [springing up] Oh I say! You don't mean that this thing is loaded, do you? My ownest: come off it.

SARAH [sitting placidly on the shell] If I am to be blown up, the more thoroughly it is done the better. Don't fuss, Cholly.

LOMAX [to Undershaft, strongly remonstrant] Your own daughter, you know.

UNDERSHAFT. So I see. [To Cusins] Well, my friend, may we expect you here at six tomorrow morning?

CUSINS [firmly] Not on any account. I will see the whole establishment blown up with its own dynamite before I will get up at five. My hours are healthy, rational hours: eleven to five.

UNDERSHAFT. Come when you please: before a week you will come at six and stay until I turn you out for the sake of your health. [Calling] Bilton! [He turns to Lady Britomart, who rises]. My dear: let us leave these two young people to themselves for a moment. [Bilton comes from the shed]. I am going to take you through the gun cotton shed.

BILTON [barring the way] You can't take anything explosive in here, Sir.

LADY BRITOMART. What do you mean? Are you alluding to me?

BILTON [unmoved] No, ma'am. Mr Undershaft has the other gentleman's matches in his pocket.

LADY BRITOMART [abruptly] Oh! I beg your pardon. [She goes into the shed].

UNDERSHAFT. Quite right, Bilton, quite right: here you are. [He gives Bilton the box of matches]. Come, Stephen. Come, Charles. Bring Sarah. [He passes into the shed].

Bilton opens the box and deliberately drops the matches into the fire-bucket.

LOMAX. Oh I say! [Bilton stolidly hands him the empty box]. Infernal nonsense! Pure scientific ignorance! [He goes in].

SARAH. Am I all right, Bilton?

BILTON. You'll have to put on list slippers, miss: that's all. We've got em inside. [She goes in].

STEPHEN [very seriously to Cusins] Dolly, old fellow, think. Think before you decide. Do you feel that you are a sufficiently practical man? It is a huge undertaking, an enormous responsibility. All this mass of business will be Greek to you.

CUSINS. Oh, I think it will be much less difficult than Greek.

STEPHEN. Well, I just want to say this before I leave you to yourselves. Don't let anything I have said about right and wrong prejudice you against this great chance in life. I have satisfied myself that the business is one of the highest character and a credit to our country. [Emotionally] I am very proud of my father. I— [Unable to proceed, he presses Cusins' hand and goes hastily into the shed, followed by Bilton].

Barbara and Cusins, left alone together, look at one another silently.

CUSINS. Barbara: I am going to accept this offer.

BARBARA. I thought you would.

CUSINS. You understand, don't you, that I had to decide without consulting you. If I had thrown the burden of the choice on you, you would sooner or later have despised me for it.

BARBARA. Yes: I did not want you to sell your soul for me any more than for this inheritance.

CUSINS. It is not the sale of my soul that troubles me: I have sold it too often to care about that. I have sold it for a professorship. I have sold it for an income. I have sold it to escape being imprisoned for refusing to pay taxes for hangmen's ropes and unjust wars and things that I abhor. What is all human conduct but the daily and hourly sale of our souls for trifles? What I am now selling it for is neither money nor position nor comfort, but for reality and for power.

BARBARA. You know that you will have no power, and that he has none.

CUSINS. I know. It is not for myself alone. I want to make power for the world.

BARBARA. I want to make power for the world too; but it must be spiritual power.

CUSINS. I think all power is spiritual: these cannons will not go off by themselves. I have tried to make spiritual power by teaching Greek. But the world can never be really touched by a dead language and a dead civilization. The people must have power; and the people cannot have Greek. Now the power that is made here can be wielded by all men.

BARBARA. Power to burn women's houses down and kill their sons and tear their husbands to pieces.

CUSINS. You cannot have power for good without having power for evil too. Even mother's milk nourishes murderers as well as heroes. This power which only tears men's bodies to pieces has never been so horribly abused as the intellectual power, the imaginative power, the poetic, religious power that can enslave men's souls. As a teacher of Greek I gave the intellectual man weapons against the common man. I now want to give the common man weapons against the intellectual man. I love the common people. I want to arm them against the lawyer, the doctor, the priest, the literary man, the professor, the artist, and the politician, who, once in authority, are the most dangerous, disastrous, and tyrannical of all the fools, rascals, and impostors. I want a democratic power strong enough to force the intellectual oligarchy to use its genius for the general good or else perish.

BARBARA. Is there no higher power than that [pointing to the shell]?

CUSINS. Yes: but that power can destroy the higher powers just as a tiger can destroy a man: therefore man must master that power first. I admitted this when the Turks and Greeks were last at war. My best pupil went out to fight for Hellas. My parting gift to him was not a copy of Plato's Republic, but a revolver and a hundred Undershaft cartridges. The blood of every Turk he shot—if he shot any—is on my head as well as on Undershaft's. That act committed me to this place for ever. Your father's challenge has beaten me. Dare I make war on war? I dare. I must. I will. And now, is it all over between us?

BARBARA [touched by his evident dread of her answer] Silly baby Dolly! How could it be?

CUSINS [overjoyed] Then you—you—you— Oh for my drum! [He flourishes imaginary drumsticks].

BARBARA [angered by his levity] Take care, Dolly, take care. Oh, if only I could get away from you and from father and from it all! if I could have the wings of a dove and fly away to heaven!

CUSINS. And leave me!

BARBARA. Yes, you, and all the other naughty mischievous children of men. But I can't. I was happy in the Salvation Army for a moment. I escaped from the world into a paradise of enthusiasm and prayer and soul saving; but the moment our money ran short, it all came back to Bodger: it was he who saved our people: he, and the Prince of Darkness, my papa. Undershaft and Bodger: their hands stretch everywhere: when we feed a starving fellow creature, it is with their bread, because there is no other bread; when we tend the sick, it is in the hospitals they endow; if we turn from the churches they build, we must kneel on the stones of the streets they pave. As long as that lasts, there is no getting away from them. Turning our backs on Bodger and Undershaft is turning our backs on life.

CUSINS. I thought you were determined to turn your back on the wicked side of life.

BARBARA. There is no wicked side: life is all one. And I never wanted to shirk my share in whatever evil must be endured, whether it be sin or suffering. I wish I could cure you of middle-class ideas, Dolly.

CUSINS [gasping] Middle cl—! A snub! A social snub to ME! from the daughter of a foundling!

BARBARA. That is why I have no class, Dolly: I come straight out of the heart of the whole people. If I were middle-class I should turn my back on my father's business; and we should both live in an artistic drawingroom, with you reading the reviews in one corner, and I in the other at the piano, playing Schumann: both very superior persons, and neither of us a bit of use. Sooner than that, I would sweep out the guncotton shed, or be one of Bodger's barmaids. Do you know what would have happened if you had refused papa's offer?

CUSINS. I wonder!

BARBARA. I should have given you up and married the man who accepted it. After all, my dear old mother has more sense than any of you. I felt like her when I saw this place—felt that I must have it—that never, never, never could I let it go; only she thought it was the houses and the kitchen ranges and the linen and china, when it was really all the human souls to be saved: not weak souls in starved bodies, crying with gratitude for a scrap of bread and treacle, but fullfed, quarrelsome, snobbish, uppish creatures, all standing on their little rights and dignities, and thinking that my father ought to be greatly obliged to them for making so much money for him—and so he ought. That is where salvation is really wanted. My father shall never throw it in my teeth again that my converts were bribed with bread. [She is transfigured]. I have got rid of the bribe of bread. I have got rid of the bribe of heaven. Let God's work be done for its own sake: the work he had to create us to do because it cannot be done by living men and women. When I die, let him be in my debt, not I in his; and let me forgive him as becomes a woman of my rank.

CUSINS. Then the way of life lies through the factory of death?

BARBARA. Yes, through the raising of hell to heaven and of man to God, through the unveiling of an eternal light in the Valley of The Shadow. [Seizing him with both hands] Oh, did you think my courage would never come back? did you believe that I was a deserter? that I, who have stood in the streets, and taken my people to my heart, and talked of the holiest and greatest things with them, could ever turn back and chatter foolishly to fashionable people about nothing in a drawingroom? Never, never, never, never: Major Barbara will die with the colors. Oh! and I have my dear little Dolly boy still; and he has found me my place and my work. Glory Hallelujah! [She kisses him].

CUSINS. My dearest: consider my delicate health. I cannot stand as much happiness as you can.

BARBARA. Yes: it is not easy work being in love with me, is it? But it's good for you. [She runs to the shed, and calls, childlike] Mamma! Mamma! [Bilton comes out of the shed, followed by Undershaft]. I want Mamma.

UNDERSHAFT. She is taking off her list slippers, dear. [He passes on to Cusins]. Well? What does she say?

CUSINS. She has gone right up into the skies.

LADY BRITOMART [coming from the shed and stopping on the steps, obstructing Sarah, who follows with Lomax. Barbara clutches like a baby at her mother's skirt]. Barbara: when will you learn to be independent and to act and think for yourself? I know as well as possible what that cry of "Mamma, Mamma," means. Always running to me!

SARAH [touching Lady Britomart's ribs with her finger tips and imitating a bicycle horn] Pip! Pip!

LADY BRITOMART [highly indignant] How dare you say Pip! pip! to me, Sarah? You are both very naughty children. What do you want, Barbara?

BARBARA. I want a house in the village to live in with Dolly. [Dragging at the skirt] Come and tell me which one to take.

UNDERSHAFT [to Cusins] Six o'clock tomorrow morning, my young friend.